Praise for
Changing What's Normal

"Most people know the phrase 'what got you here won't get you there.' So why is it many still can't 'get there'?   It's because they are not changing what's normal. I will be forever indebted to Ian for sharing his insights with me and guiding me through the journey of Changing What's Normal.   Straight talking and no bull (what do you expect from an Aussie!)
Changing What's Normal helped me to move from the 'how to' guy to
the 'go to' guy."
Kwai Yu, Founder and CEO of Leaders Cafe

"I strongly recommend this book to people who share a passion for making the world a better place through collaboration, shared values, noble objectives and a desire to get the very best out of the people around them and as a consequence out of themselves."
Terry McGivern, Executive Team member, Smurfit Kappa UK

"This book is full of valuable insights and thought-provoking questions that truly go beyond the normal business platitudes; and invite and challenge YOU to change what's normal in your life and your organisation."
Gihan Perera, Business Strategist

"Ian Berry is NOT NORMAL – and that's a compliment.   Normal is not the behavior that the world needs from you right now.   Read Ian's book to take a look at yourself and learn some straightforward ideas you can use to add a bit of abnormal to your life."
Julie Poland, corporate coach, speaker, and author of *Changing Results by Changing Behavior*.

"In my opinion anyone picking up this easy to read book could only find it a valuable resource but more importantly a reflective personal development tool for all aspects of their life."
Gary Anderson, Strategic Marketing Director, Tucker Creative

"This is a book that will be a constant reference on my desk - whether applying to myself and my business or to that of clients'. Change what's normal?   The days of normal are always yesterday.   The day of change is today.   Tomorrow is the beneficiary of that change.   Ian Berry's practical insights and helpful tools present anyone reading this with an opportunity to change, to lead and to grow. Perhaps it is time that we embrace "abnormal"."
Richard Norris, Serendipity Global Ltd

Changing What's Normal

Ian Berry

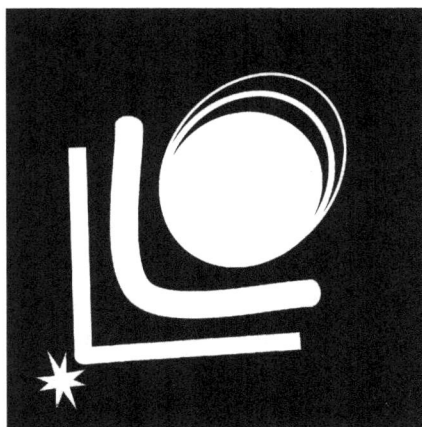

Published by Customer Centred Consulting Pty Ltd
Australia

The author welcomes conversation about any aspects of this book.

www.changingwhatsnormal.com
email: ian@changingwhatsnormal.com
Phone: +61 418 807 898

National Library of Australia
Cataloguing-in-Publication data
Berry, Ian
Changing What's Normal
ISBN 978-0-9581236-3-1

First published in Australia in 2011.
Second Edition May 2013
Reprinted 2020

For Carol,
the great sparkenation in my life
and for everyone who is
or wants to be
a differencemaker

**I believe every human being wants
and deserves to be loved, valued, and fulfilled.
Imagine our world when everyone is.**

When I made this statement in a speech once
a guy yelled out:
"He believes in Utopia" and laughed out loud.

I don't believe in Utopia.

I do believe in possibility.

Nothing changes until we believe in possibility.

Once upon a time 30 years was the normal life expectancy for humans.

It was once normal to take 6 months to travel from one side of the world to the other.

It was once normal to believe that there was no cure for many diseases that have now been eradicated.

No change is possible unless ...

From a distance Barack Obama seems to me to be a warm, wise, and wonderful human being, and one of the most articulate people of his generation, perhaps of all time.

He was given a Nobel Peace Prize based on what he might do, rather than on what he had done, in my view. It is a false hope unless ...

Despite his personal significance Barack Obama is primarily powerless to change what is normal in our world.
His *"Yes we can"* has become *"No we can't"*, unless ...

In an excellent book, a New York Times No. 1 bestseller *Switch - how to change things when change is hard,* the authors Chip and Dan Heath propose a great three-phase process for change: direct our rational mind, motivate our emotional side, and shape the path of change. Their book is about behaviour change that will rarely happen unless ...

Most training or change programs undertaken by millions of people every day fail to lead to behaviour change unless ...

The unless I refer to is: **unless intention changes.**

The Republican politicians in the United States of America's parliament have an intention, it seems to me, to replace Barack Obama, a Democrat, with one of their own. This intention drives everything they do.

The members of the Liberal/Nationals coalition party in my home country, Australia, have the same intent. They want one of their own as our Prime Minister, and it drives everything they do.

This kind of intention has political parties, not in government, all over the world by the throat, and we are all choking as a result.

This kind of intention means good, sound ideas, put forward by politicians in power, rarely see the light of day and compromise and inaction is the result. (I wrote this section in June 2011. Sadly the status quo remains).

Success depends on where intention is. Right now the political intentions of most are in the wrong place and, therefore, we are heading as a human race to the wrong place.

Consider just two facts, undisputed by any thinking person:
1. How most of us live in the world is unsustainable.
2. More than 6 million children under the age of five die every year, that's 16,000 per day, simply because they do not have the right nutrition.

We have the solutions to both these problems and many others we are failing to solve. Why have we failed? We have failed because the intention of most is about I rather than we, which means winners and losers.

Changing What's Normal is about changing our intention to one where everyone can win. Intention is another word for purpose.

If your intention or purpose is to co-create a world where everyone can win, to co-create change people can actually believe in, and make happen, then you will gain much from this book, providing you do your work.

How to gain the most from this book

Please note that I use the words organisation and business interchangeably.

I share with you 58 sparkenations.
I created '**sparkenation**' to describe: **a spark that ignites passion that leads to action that changes what's normal.**

I recommend you read my book from start to finish and then go back and explore wherever you feel moved to go. My suggestion is to work on one sparkenation at a time until you have changed what's normal. Some will obviously take you longer than others.

Many of my sparkenations have been gleaned from my work, since 1991, with enlightened and passionate business leaders, in several countries, seeking to thrive on the challenges of change.

I begin each sparkenation by stating what I feel/think is currently normal and then the rest of the sparkenation is about how you could change what's normal.

At the end of each sparkenation are possibility action/s you can decide on taking so that you actually change what's normal in your own way.

At the beginning of all of my presentations I tell my audiences: "What I have to say is not important, rather what you hear yourself say to yourself, that's what's important."

I finish each sparkenation with the words **"do your work"** because it is not what I have said or suggested that is important. What is really important is what you intend, feel and think, and then what you actually do.

The words *Do Your Work* are the title of an excellent book by Steven Pressfield about overcoming resistance. Steven believes that the pain of running away from doing what we know we should is greater than actually doing the work!

There is a link to a great, short video by Steven in the **online learning vault that is a companion to this book.** The vault contains downloadable files, references, links, tools, tips, techniques, templates. Each time I refer to the vault I do so in the possibility action/s section. You may like to bookmark this page www.changingwhatsnormal.com/vault/ for easy access.

I will share stories throughout of several defining moments in my life. We each have defining moments. When we live the lessons we learn through these moments we change what's normal and inspire others to do the same.

"The best story isn't my story or your story; the best story is our story" says Mark Sanborn. Therefore the best stories we tell are those other people recognise themselves in.

As you recognise yourself in my stories, my request of you is that you will reflect and then decide to be more of who you are capable of becoming, and do your work. The world needs the best you have got right now, today.

Sparkenations

Action 2: Change Your Relationships.   81
Relationship change follows personal change.
Connect, Commune, Collaborate.

Sparkenations 24 - 28

Action 1.
Change yourself.

All change is personal first:
Sparkenations 1 - 23

**Change
Yourself**

Discover
Distinguish
Develop
Differentiate
Deliver

Discover: Sparkenations 1 - 6

"The real voyage of discovery consists not in seeking new landscapes, but in having new eyes."
Marcel Proust

The six sparkenations in this section are about having new eyes.

I know people who have changed hairstyle, diet, partners, jobs, cities, countries, and in some cases, all of these, yet still summarise their life in the words of the U2 song: *"I still haven't found what I'm looking for."*

We need to be brave and look long in the mirror and if we do not like who we see, then it is high time to change what's normal.

For me our knowing-doing gap, a false picture we have of ourselves, doing what we've always done, our dogma, our thinking that our way is the only way, or the non-discovery of our life's work, or perhaps all six, conspire to create a picture of ourselves, that isn't who we really are.

We need new eyes.

Sparkenation 1.
Closing your knowing-doing gap

There are many great insights in Daniel Pink's book *Drive – the surprising truth about what motivate us.* One of Daniel's conclusions really made me think: *"there is a mismatch between what science knows and business does."*

Normal

There is a mismatch for most of us between what we know and what we do.

Changing What's Normal

For me the narrower the gap between what we know and what we do, the more fulfilled life we live and the greater influence we assert.

Part of my plan in 2011, my 20th in partnering with passionate and enlightened business leaders to change what's normal inside organisations for the good of people, our planet, and for profit, is to close the gap between what I know and what I do.

I am finding this challenging!

The most demanding aspect of my work with organisations is to inspire people to actually do what they know they should, and I too am not finding this easy.

To begin my own journey to close my gap, I reread *The Knowing-Doing Gap* by J. Pfeffer and R.I. Sutton (HBS Press, 1999), a very insightful book.

From there I made a list of the crucial things I know about life and business where I have have not fully implemented, or acted on successfully, what I know.

Possibility action:

Try the above exercise, i.e. make your own list.

I am sure you too will find actioning your list challenging, however, like me, as you change what's normal, you will find the journey as rewarding as I am.

"To know and not to do is really not to know."
attributed to Stephen R. Covey in some circles and simply as Zen wisdom in other places.

My strong desire is that this book will inspire you deeply to make the gap between what you know and what you do as narrow as you possibly can.

Do your work.

Sparkenation 2.
I'm not normal and neither are you

Normal

Most people hold an inaccurate image of themselves that is much to do with what they think other people think about them. Sadly this kind of self-image can last a lifetime.

Changing What's Normal

The biggest message I heard from my teachers at school, when I was a teenager, was that I was stupid. A common phrase from many of them was: *"What are you doing, stupid?"*

On Sundays in those years I heard a different message, *"You are a sinner in need of redemption."*

On many Saturdays I heard yet another message.

After sport on Saturday mornings I would often visit my Grandparents on my way home. My Nana Sherriff, whose shepherds pie I can still smell and taste whenever I think about it, often used to look across her kitchen table and say, *"You know you're special!"*

I didn't know who I was, and strangely enough, when I look back, I wonder why I chose stupid as the picture I had of myself most of the time.

When I left school the only job I could get was working as a brickie's labourer for a construction firm owned by friends of my family, a firm my Grandfather Sherriff worked for until his death at age 76. I also worked for a time as a painter for another friend of my family.

One day I was painting a church, the same place where I'd heard over and over that I was a sinner. My mother's friend, Mrs. Murray, who lived across the road, came to get me, on this particular day, because another friend of the family wanted to talk to me on the telephone. There were no mobile phones in the 70s!

Noel, who worked for a recruitment organisation, was calling to tell me he had an interview for me with the National Australia Bank, and that I needed to cut off my long hair, shave off my beard, buy a suit (I didn't own one at the time), and to do so quickly.

The only good thing my school report card said was, *"Ian has a sense of humour"*, so my interviewer didn't waste any time cutting to the chase saying, *"There is no way I could give you a job son, I'm sorry."*

I thought *"I've got nothing to lose"* and replied, *"I am not going to get on my hands and knees and beg, however I promise you, if you give me a chance, I won't let you down."*

My interviewer then shocked me when he reached out, shook my hand, and said, *"You're hired!"*

A few days later when I started work, my hirer, who became my first mentor, told me he wasn't sure what came over him, saying, *"I just had the feeling you were someone special!"*

So Nana Sherriff was right and for the first time in my life, at age 17, I believed her and I have never looked back.

Deep down I always knew I wasn't normal. The reason I got into so much trouble at school was because I felt other people were forcing me to be like everyone else and I rebelled.

I was fortunate that my first employer in the business world didn't think I was normal either. His mentoring taught me that my quest in life was to be the best one-of-a-kind that I could be and that authentic leadership is about creating cultures where everyone has opportunity to shine.

My first mentor had a great philosophy which I later discovered was popularised by Goethe, the great German philosopher:

> *When we treat man as he is, we make him worse than he is;*
> *when we treat him as if he already were*
> *what he potentially could be,*
> *we make him what he should be.*
> Goethe

Sadly very few of the so-called educators I experienced in my youth understood the truth of these words.

I have been fortunate to work with some remarkable people who get Goethe's truth, and I have been honoured to meet several more.

Are you such a person?

Possibility actions:

How normal do you see yourself?

Could you be more of a non-conformist?
If so what would you do differently and when will you begin?

How often do you celebrate that you are special?
Could you do so more often?

How often do you see people as they could be and celebrate the special nature of every human being with individuals?

Could you do so more often?

Do your work.

Sparkenation 3.
History is not my story or yours

Normal

History has a habit of repeating itself.

In the few hours that I watch television and read newspapers each week I am staggered by the amount of times I see, hear, and read the same story in various contexts, particularly when it comes to politics, religion, and business. We seem to be making the same mistakes over and over and over again and don't learn from making them.

This reoccurring nightmare happens because our intentions, feelings, and thoughts, and therefore, our behaviour, hasn't changed.

Changing What's Normal

One way to tackle this historical problem is to realise that history doesn't have to be our story. We must learn from history, indeed honour history. Our quest then is to resolve and act so that we do not make the same mistakes. We can literally change the course of history by being different.

My first real experience of history repeating itself happened when I realised I was making the same mistakes as a parent, with my children, that my parents had made with me. I modified my intent, feelings and thoughts about being a parent and over time my new actions bettered my relationship with my kids.

My major experience of history repeating itself however came about when I realised I had become the kind of boss I had once despised!

As I changed my ways, I saw my employees change their ways as well and together we created a new story.

Possibility action:

At home, at work, in all aspects of your life, how are you repeating history and what would you need to modify or change to ensure the negative aspects of history are not your story?

Reflect. Decide.

Do your work.

Sparkenation 4.
Is your progress being
delayed by dogma?

Normal

"Dogma is living with the results of other people's thinking",
said Steve Jobs the co-founder of Apple.

Changing What's Normal

A big shift happened for me, in changing what's normal and living
a life at peace with myself, being happy, and living in harmony
with other people and our planet, when I let go my rule book and
stopped being a prisoner to the belief systems of others.   Beliefs
that I really deep down inside did not believe.

In a session with a mentor, one time, she asked me **if I was
willing to give up my rule book?** I was, however, I found it very
hard to do!

There are rules in society that are there primarily to protect us and
fellow beings from ourselves and each other.   Otherwise there
would be so much more chaos than there already is that we would
probably cease to exist.

We have our own rules as well however.

My rule book used to say:

- ✓ Nobody should give bad service so I should tell people off
  when they do.
- ✓ If I think something is wrong I'd better fix it before it gets
  worse.

✓ Before this or that gets off the rails I should say something to 'help' (and I used to say it).

✓ I should be appreciated more often.

✓ People don't deserve to be treated poorly and if I don't do anything about it nobody will.

✓ People who don't reply to emails should be sanctioned.

I could go on and on. I once had a lot of rules!

My mentor pointed out to me that my rules are often fantasy or completely irrelevant or unknown for others.

I spent a lot of time and energy thinking about this and I agree with my mentor. I have thrown out my rule book.

I have learnt that what is, is. I am learning that the more I accept this and not try to control things, judge others, or 'make things better', which is what my rule book used to be all about, I am much more peaceful, powerful, inspirational, and many times more effective.

Instead of my rules I now focus on rules of engagement when the possibility of collaborating or engaging with others presents itself.

The best rules of engagement are those we have agreed to work with, which means building a relationship with others really matters before we can properly engage.

Have you got your own rule book?

Maybe if you discarded it your life would be better. I can't comment. What you do is none of my business.

An email from a colleague David Bernard-Stevens from USA on December 10th 2010 turned into a defining moment for me. Thank you David.

In David's email he referred to a project that we were working as not being joyful. I took this to my heart because he was right.

In May 2009 on a trip to New Zealand with friends Lindsay Adams, his wife Debby, and my wife Carol, I lost the plot (that's Aussie for behaving badly) due to some travel issues. Not only did I upset myself, I also upset everyone in close proximity.

Since that day, my mantra has been to *"show up joyful"*, initially to do with travel, which is a major part of my life, and eventually to do with everything. I had always been annoyed at Woody Allen's edict *"80% of success is showing up"*. For me it is how we show up that really matters, and so my life's mantra became *"show up joyful!"*

In the latter part of 2010 joy had disappeared from much of my work albeit not concerning travel, I am happy to say I have mastered that one! (I still have the occasional glitch, no one is perfect, right?) I recognised a pattern in my life - I go really hard and full on at things and get annoyed with people who don't do what I think they should, particularly when they have made a commitment or what I perceive is a commitment. This has been a rule in my life that has taken me a while to break.

I am still doing what I love to do in the service of people who love what I do - writing, speaking, mentoring, conducting 'changing what's normal' programs with passionate people, and collaborating with others on projects that solve world problems. My desire is that I will be able to keep doing these things until my last breath, however, I have let go of the labour bit which, for me, is about my feelings when people don't do what I feel they have committed to do or don't do what I think they should do.

To finally put a full stop to this has been amazing. I feel 10 years younger!

And what of your beliefs around your rules?
This is what I call dogma.

On letting go my rule book I was then able, over time, to let go of certain beliefs I'd held about others, particularly about what I thought was right and wrong, and my wanting to be right. The freedom of knowing my way in life is as legitimate as anyone else's and that there is no right or wrong way is exhilarating and opens the door to a deeply fulfilling life.

Possibility Action:

Examine closely what you believe about what you believe and make a decision today to let go. And then, let go.

Do your work.

Sparkenation 5.
One solution to the world's pre-eminent problem

Normal

Fundamentalists are killing us, literally. In my view fundamentalists are people who believe their way is the only way.

Today these folk of religious, political, business, and other persuasions are ruining our world. None of us has a mortgage on truth. And none of us has a right to use violence against anybody for any reason, let alone because we believe something different or are following a different path.

Changing What's Normal

In the new world being co-created we will honour everyone's path to meaning, whatever it is, and we will be tolerant of another person's way and co-exist regardless of our differences, indeed we will celebrate our differences.

We live in three worlds: the world in here, the world out there, and the world we share. In here, our views are just that, out there are other people's views. In the world we share are the views we agree on. In any successful relationship the world we share is the critical one.

Human conflict is fundamentally the result of failure to agree on the goal or failure to agree on the strategies to achieve the goal.

I guarantee that today all of our troubles, personal, local, organisational, national, and international, are fundamentally based in our perceived need to hang onto the world in here, our issues with the world out there, and, our failure to focus more on the world we share.

What makes life really worthwhile is when we can share our views (without ridiculing one another or being violent with one another) and come together with a shared view, which may mean we have to let go of things we previously held dear.

I trust that today and every day you will resolve to build more of the world we share and be less precious about the world in here or the world out there.

Possibility Action:

Decide right now to be a more of a builder of a world that is based on shared view.

What modifications or changes would you need to make in your life to make this happen?

Get started today on making the changes you have decided to make.

Do your work.

Sparkenation 6.
Discovering your life's work

Normal

Most people are not doing what they love in the service of people who love what they do. Instead most of us are doing what we think we must in order to get by.

Changing What's Normal

The work and example of Joseph Campbell, Daniel Pink, Ken Robinson, Steven Farber, and Benjamin Zander have had a huge impact on my life.

I designed the 16 statements that follow as a result of their inspiration to help you discover what you love to do and then to do that in the service of people who will love what you do.

Possibility Actions:

Consider each statement on the following pages and give yourself a rating out of 10 regarding your current situation. A 10 would mean you are doing what the statement says with all you've got.

A lesser rating suggests a performance gap and therefore work for you to do to close the gap. Do your work and discover your life's work, and as Benjamin Zander would say, your *"shining eyes"*.

Section 1: **Can Do**

1. I am using the most important things I know in my work

In rating this statement think about what you know about people, systems, and the actions you take outside of the workplace that work for you. How you are applying your life's principles and values at work.

2. I get to use my key skills daily

In rating this statement think about what you are competent at and what you are outstanding at, across your life. How much you are using what you are good at in your role/s at work.

3. I can express my expertise freely and openly

In rating this statement think about what you do that others would say you are really good at.

4. I know my limitations and what I still need to learn to be remarkable

In rating this statement think about the gap between what you know and what you do, as well as the skills you still need to learn or the attitudes you need to adopt to really excel in your work on a consistent basis.

Section 2: **Will Do**

5. I maintain a great attitude to my life and work

In rating this statement think about how grateful you are when things go according to plan and when they don't. Think how much you take responsibility for your feelings, thoughts, and actions and don't take responsibility for other people's feelings, thoughts, and actions. Think also about how much you live in the now, how much you celebrate when you succeed as well as fail, and how much you complain or whine.

6. I work weekly for at least one cause that is greater than myself

In rating this statement think about the charities, non-profits, associations, or causes you support and how much time and energy and/or money you give to these.

7. I am disciplined in turning feelings and thoughts into action

In rating this statement think about how many feelings and thoughts you actually act on compared to feelings and thoughts you don't act on.

8. I can articulate how what I do differentiates me from others

In rating this statement think about what you do that is different, better, or more unique than what others in the same or similar role/s to you do.

Section 3: Love to Do

9. I am very clear on what my purpose in life is

In rating this statement think about why you do what you do and why you are who you are. Think about your reasons for doing what you do and what legacy you will have left when you are gone.

10. People who know me know what I passionate about

In rating this statement think about what your best friends would say that you are passionate about or really care about. Think also about what really excites you and what you are enthusiastic about and, if you had a choice to do whatever you could, what would you be doing?

11. I can articulate what makes me joyful in a few sentences

In rating this statement think about what really brings joy to your life and to the lives of people you care about.

12. I can express my art (what comes naturally) in many different ways

In rating this statement think about all of the skills that come naturally to you, what you do well without thinking. If someone asked you to say what you are really good at, what would be your answer?

Section 4: People Who Love What I Do

13. I see serving others as the easiest way to meet my own needs

In rating this statement think about the people who get your work next. When you are done with something, who gets it next and do those people see you as providing them with a service that is valuable to them and how many people reciprocate by providing you with good service?

14. I help other people achieve what is important to them

In rating this statement think about how much you know about what is really important to other people and how much you are helping others to achieve what is important to them.

15. I know precisely how I help people solve their problems

In rating this statement think about how many times a week people thank you for helping them and how many times a week people come to you and ask you for help in solving something with them.

16. I offer a myriad of solutions that can help others overcome their challenges

In rating this statement think about how many different ways you have helped different people to solve the same problem and how observant you are in offering solutions to people in ways that they will see as valuable and not a 'put down' of them.

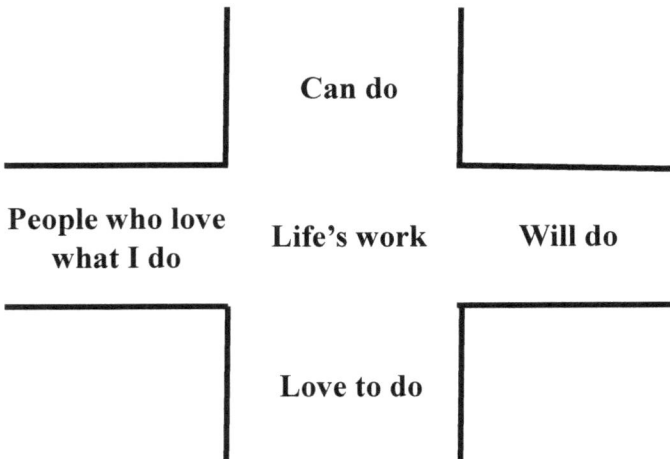

Can do

People who love what I do   **Life's work**   **Will do**

Love to do

Further Possibility Action:

There is a link in the vault www.changingwhatsnormal.com/vault/ to a TED talk by Benjamin Zander. Please watch and reflect on Ben's concept of *"shining eyes"*. Work out what it means to you and make some changes to your life.

Don't just watch; reflect, decide.

Do your work.

Distinguish: Sparkenations 7 - 10

It is estimated that 106 billion people have been born since the dawn of the human race.

And not one of us is the same as anyone else.

Yet few of us really distinguish ourselves despite the fact that none of us is normal.

Paying close attention to several key factors and taking action results in us being able to distinguish ourselves more than through just our biological differences. These factors are:

- ✓ Our defining moments, what we learn from them, and how we live the lessons.

- ✓ Our ability and willingness to understand what triggers our worst behaviour and to turn such occasions into opportunities for growth.

- ✓ Our ability to recognise when we need to change our behaviour and our willingness to change and to seek input from others as to what we should do.

- ✓ Knowing our true character and being prepared to live according to it no matter what the situation.

Sparkenations 7 - 10 take a closer look at these factors.

Sparkenation 7.
Living our lessons from 9/11

Normal

Most people respond to something bad happening to them with revenge and fail to grasp the opportunity to do good.

Changing What's Normal

My grandson Hamish was born a week after 9/11. On 9/11, the day my daughter was due to give birth, my wife was in Perth with our daughter and I was at home in Adelaide with a flight booked to fly to Perth on the 13th. That night, my wife and I spoke on the telephone about what kind of a world our first grandchild was likely to grow up in.

On the day of my scheduled flight, the airline I had booked on, Ansett, then an iconic Australian company, suddenly closed down. I was not able to get a flight on another airline, or a seat on a train or bus, so I got in my car and drove to Perth, a 36 hour drive. What occupied my mind for much of that trip was the question, *"what is the purpose of my life?"*

I couldn't even begin (still can't) to imagine the horror for those who died in the World Trade Center and the devastation for their families, yet it inspired me to think deeply about my own life, and how I could do more to make a difference in the world.

The long drive to Perth was full of defining moments for me where I made decisions that still drive my life and my work.

When I held the precious new life of my Grandson in my arms for the first time I realised that what was becoming 'normal' in our world, at that time, was not the sort of normal world that I wanted him to grow up in. I made a silent promise to do everything in my power to never accept 'normal' when that means that less than what is possible is happening in our world.

This book is part of my action plan. It's a big task and I am just one person. I am asking for your help. I am asking you to do your work, so that together we might co-create a world where everyone can win and nobody loses.

In 2005 my wife and I were in London partly due to my work and partly for holidays. We traveled on the London Underground the day after the terrorist attack on that rail system. You could feel the fear and yet also the resolve of travellers to not be beaten by people who commit terrorist acts. This experience was another defining moment for me in my life.

What have been your life's defining moments?

I have had many defining moments, some big like those events mentioned above, and some small, yet significant, moments that have inspired me to change what's normal about my life.

Possibility Actions:

Big and small, what have been your defining moments?
What have been the key lessons of these moments?
And how are you living your lessons today?

In the online learning vault, that is a companion to this book, there is an exercise you can undertake anytime you wish to review your defining moments and how you are living the lessons today.
You can access it at www.changingwhatsnormal.com/vault/
Do your work.

Sparkenation 8.
When our worst triggers our best

Normal

Most of us do not recognise what triggers our worst behaviour and as a consequence we miss many opportunities for growth.

Changing What's Normal

As I have mentioned, I have sometimes allowed travel to bring out the worst in me! On a recent trip I read a wonderful book called *The Way We're Working Isn't Working* by Tony Schwartz with Jean Gomes and Catherine McCarthy, Ph.D.   I pondered pages 139 and 140 carefully, for here the authors outline the following triggers of our worst behaviour and suggest that most come from a feeling of being devalued.

Feeling spoken to with condescension or lack of respect

Being treated unfairly

Not feeling appreciated

Not being listened to or feeling heard

Someone else taking credit for my work

Being kept waiting

Someone else's sloppy work on a project I'm overseeing

Unrealistic deadlines

People who think they know it all

I identify with most of these! How about you?

Possibility Actions:

Determine what triggers you and change how you normally respond so that you are no longer triggered.

Ask yourself how are you devaluing other people by behaving in ways that trigger their worst behaviour? Stop doing what you currently do.

Do your work.

Sparkenation 9.
Feedforward is often more powerful
than feedback

Normal

Most feedback we get, we didn't ask for and often it comes hidden in a velvet glove of somebody appearing to be nice, yet really, they are simply trying to change us to be more like them.

Changing What's Normal

To inspire and encourage personal change, all of my initial work, when I partner with clients on change projects, is to help individuals change intention, feelings and thinking before even contemplating behaviour change.

I start with the leadership team and as people begin to make intention, feeling, and thinking changes, the behaviour changes that are needed start to become obvious.   I then introduce Marshall Goldsmith's *feedforward* exercise to facilitate the beginnings of behaviour change. I highly recommend Marshall's book *What Got You Here Won't Get You There* which details *feedforward* and many other great ideas that inspire personal change.

Feedforward is often more powerful than feedback.

Individuals:

1. Pick one behaviour they would like to change

2. They describe their objective with someone 1:1

3. They then ask that person for two suggestions for the future that might help them achieve their objective.
   The only response to give to people who give feedforward is *"Thank You!"*

Sometimes people need encouragement to identify the behaviour changes they need to make.

Marshall Goldsmith's *20 transactional flaws* can help with with such identification.

1. *Winning too much*
2. *Adding too much value*
3. *Passing judgement*
4. *Making destructive comments*
5. *Starting with "No," "But," or "However"*
6. *Telling the world how smart you are*
7. *Speaking when angry*
8. *Negativity, or "Let me explain why that won't work"*
9. *Withholding information*
10. *Failing to give proper recognition*
11. *Claiming credit that we don't deserve*
12. *Making excuses*
13. *Clinging to the past*
14. *Playing favourites*
15. *Refusing to express regret*
16. *Not listening*
17. *Failing to express gratitude*
18. *Punishing the messenger*
19. *Passing the buck*
20. *An excessive need to be 'me'*

Possibility Action:

Feedforward is a very powerful exercise.

Do your work.

There is a link in the vault www.changingwhatsnormal.com/vault/ to Marshall Goldsmith's library of wonderful resources including a video about *feedforward* and an online assessment that only takes about 10 minutes to complete.

I heard Marshall speak in New York in August 2008 at the National Speakers Association Convention and was impressed, not just with his delivery, I was also inspired by his generosity in encouraging people to use his tools.

Warning:
Work on intention, feeling, and thinking change **before** behaviour change.

Sparkenation 10.
Where have all the people
of character gone?

Normal

Heavy storm clouds stay hanging over business, religion, politics, sport, and the media. Almost daily many so-called 'icons' are continuing to have their character questioned. These clouds always produce rain and wash away the 'stars' like twigs in a river.

Changing What's Normal

Like never before the world needs ordinary people of character to stand up and be counted because many of the people leading us don't understand leadership, have sacrificed their character in their quest for power, and in some cases, their behaviour threatens our very lives.

Recently the father of a good friend passed on. He was a man of character and an inspiration to my friend. His passing caused me to reflect on my own father who passed more than a decade ago.

Like my friend's father, my dad never had his name up in lights too often but left a legacy to be proud of in his world nonetheless. I miss him. Dad was a man of character. We never always saw eye to eye. It was the words of the Mike and the Mechanics song *In the Living Years* that urged me to settle my differences with Dad not long before he died.

"It's too late when you die", the song says, *"to admit you don't see eye to eye."*

Towards the end, Dad came to hear me speak. Before I began he announced publicly: *"I probably won't agree with everything the speaker says this morning, but I am proud that he is my son."*

People of character lay it on the line like that.

People of character are unafraid to speak their minds.

People of character always tell the truth as they see it.

People of character are trustworthy.

People of character have integrity.

People of character enjoy being popular but don't seek popularity.

People of character seek win/win but do not compromise their principles.

People of character do what they believe is best for the common good regardless of the resistance they encounter.

People of character praise in public and offer critique in private.

People of character are givers not takers.

People of character focus on building people's self esteem and never engage in 'put downs' or the blame and shame game.

People of character are those we really look up to and admire.

People of character are those we follow when it matters most.

Be a person of character. You are needed like never before.

Possibility Actions:

Ask 10 people who know you well, and whose opinion you respect, to rate your behaviour out of 10 in each of my insights above about what people of character do. Take immediate remedial action on any behaviour where people rate you at less than 10.

Another option is to use the concept of *feedforward* explored previously.

Do your work.

Develop: Sparkenations 11 - 14

All personal change is preceded by development work on ourselves.

There are thirteen keys to self development.

Ten are explored in Sparkenation 11 which is about stepping up to your personal significance.

The other three, explored in Sparkenations 12, 13, and 14, are:

✓ the rituals we undertake daily, fortnightly, monthly, quarterly, and yearly.

✓ the decision we make to step up and claim our personal significance.

✓ the calculated risks we take.

Sparkenation 11.
Stepping up to personal significance

Normal

Most people work hard on things that don't really matter.
I often call this *"majoring in minors."*

Changing What's Normal

One of my heroes, Jim Rohn, passed on 5th December 2009, my wife's birthday.

I was very fortunate to meet Jim on two occasions and to participate in his seminars on five occasions. I have also listened to many of his audio recordings over and over and read many of his books, however the words he uttered the very first time I heard him speak are still at the forefront of my mind:

"Work harder on yourself than you do on your job."

My friend, and one of Australia's most sought after speakers, Keith Abraham says:

"If you are not investing in yourself then you are a poor judge of a great investment."

How much time, energy and money are you investing in developing and growing yourself?

If your answer is not significant then I know, from working with a myriad of entrepreneurs, SME owners, and leaders in several countries since 1991, that your business is not achieving anywhere near what it could be.

Self development precedes all other development.

Possibility Actions:

There are a zillion ways we can become all that we are capable of becoming.

Here are 10:

1. Read books/book summaries or listen to audio recordings of books.

My colleague Geoff McDonald is the Book Rapper. He puts together short, meaty summaries that take very little time to read. His details along with my list of recommended books to read are in the online learning vault
www.changingwhatsnormal.com/vault/

Take the following actions during and from your reading/ listening:

   a. as you read/listen, write down how you can take action on the insights you are gleaning.
   b. review your notes and decide on one or two things you can incorporate into your life and work.
   c. do your work!

2. Work with a mentor regularly

Choose people who have the skills listed on the next page and spend at least three sessions with your mentor over a period of time.

✓ the ability and willingness to ask questions and the self discipline to not necessarily give answers.

✓ the ability and willingness to actively and reflectively listen and a willingness to understand in non-judgmental and non-prejudicial ways.

✓ the ability and willingness to engage in dialogue that inspires others to take action in their own way.

✓ the ability and willingness to share experience in ways others will find valuable in making their own decisions and taking action in their own way.

✓ the ability and willingness to be silent as others focus and think through their issues.

✓ the ability and willingness to give sound advice but more to encourage people to find their own way forward.

I work with a mentor at least twice a year and I choose people, who I know from my research, will take me out of my comfort zones.

3. Mentor others

I learn so much when I give of myself to others. Of recent times I have been inspired by Steven Farber's work *Greater Than Yourself* and so I work with several people with the sole purpose that they will do greater things than I and that then they will repeat the process with others.

There are more details in the vault
www.changingwhatsnormal.com/vault/

"The secret of happiness is to find something more important than you are, and then dedicate your life to it."
Daniel Dennett

4. Belong to a peer or mastermind group

I first learned about mastermind groups from the book *Think and Grow Rich* by Napoleon Hill, a book every leader should read again and again.

Join groups where you are the only member who does what you do. I find these groups of greater value than those where everyone is in the same line of work.

5. Participate in a blend of seminars/workshops/webinars/ elearning and apply your learning in your work as soon as it is practical to do so

6. Invest in time wisely (the next sparkenation may help you)

7. Subscribe to ezines and podcasts

8. Join communities where you can engage online and in person

9. Keep a journal of what works for you. You will find this a handy reference when things don't go according to plan

10. Go to the movies and live shows regularly. Movies and theatre provide great insights into what is and what can be.

Do your work.

Sparkenation 12.
Crossing the discipline bridge

Normal

Most of us lack discipline and therefore don't do what we know we should.

Changing What's Normal

Another of Jim Rohn's great insights:
"Discipline is the bridge between thought and accomplishment."

I have the honour and privilege of mentoring people in several countries. One tool I share with many is the rituals I keep daily, weekly, fortnightly, monthly, quarterly, and yearly. I encourage my clients to create their own rituals document and many report back that it helps them immeasurably to wisely invest in time and to achieve the actions essential to achieve their goals.

Possibility action:

Download my rituals one pager in the online learning vault at www.changingwhatsnormal.com/vault/

Create your own rituals document, follow it to the letter, and I am certain you will change much of what is normal in your life for the better.

Do your work.

Sparkenation 13.
The Rise of the Social Entrepreneur
and Intrapreneur

Normal

For me there are, broadly speaking, three kinds of people that I meet in the modern organisation:

The happy being miserable: these folk complain about everything and are disengaged from their work. It is not that these people aren't good people, they just haven't found their place as yet.

The happy being mediocre: these folk sit in silence, however they are open to inspiration and influence, and therefore can be engaged.

The happy being magnificent: these folk refuse to complain about anything and are fully engaged in their work.

For years the typical organisation's people engagement percentages have been: 10% miserable, 80% mediocre, and 10% magnificent.

Changing What's Normal

The happy being magnificent are on the rise. I have had the great privilege and honour to work with many of these folk. Often they have been part of the *'change champions'* team that has emerged after consultation and exploration with stakeholders about desired changes and a shared view has been reached about what will be changed.

The happy being magnificent have had enough of fake leadership and have taken their destiny in their own hands. In some circles they are being referred to as *"social intrapreneurs"*.

"I am convinced we are about to go over the awareness tipping zone", says Bill Drayton of Ashoka, *"to an 'everyone a changemaker' world."*

The happy being magnificent have a sense of self that is inspiring:

- ✓ I am a one-of-kind. Therefore I am obligated to be the best I can be.
- ✓ I can't wait for other people to take action. I will do what I can regardless of what others do or don't do.
- ✓ I will do today what others won't be doing until tomorrow.
- ✓ I am doing what I love to do in the service of others.
- ✓ I know my life's work and I am fulfilling it.
- ✓ I live with passion.
- ✓ I am responsible for my own feelings, thoughts, and actions.
- ✓ I know it is not what happens that is important, rather how I respond to what happens.
- ✓ I don't judge how others live their lives I simply follow my own path.
- ✓ I am aware of my talents and I am putting them to good use.
- ✓ I know my shortcomings and collaborate with others who have strengths that I do not.
- ✓ I maintain *an attitude of gratitude* no matter what.
- ✓ What I do matters. I make a difference.

Possibility Actions:

Are you happy being miserable, mediocre, or magnificent?

Decide to be magnificent today and every day. Step up to your personal significance. Stop doing anything miserable or mediocre that you currently do.

Do your work.

For more on 'Social Intrapreneurs and Entrepreneurs' please visit the vault at www.changingwhatsnormal.com/vault/

Sparkenation 14.
There are rarely rewards
without first taking risks

Normal

Most people play it safe because they don't want to rock the boat for fear of losing something they treasure or feel they need.

I have often wondered why many politicians who were very successful prior to entering politics become but mere shadows of themselves inside politics.

One of my answers to this is that they stop taking risks for fear of losing their seats!

Compromise is the result. Compromise rarely achieves anything great. Politics where there is the Government, an Opposition, and a few Independents and minor parties, like in Australia, fails to understand that success in the 21st century is about collaboration not compromise.

Changing What's Normal

Co-promises rather than compromise work. And they are the result of collaboration. Effective collaboration requires risk.

Right now the world is stalled on fundamental changes required in economics, managing our climate, human rights, and a host of other issues where change is urgent, because we lack risk takers and are being lead by compromisers.

To get to the point of achieving a co-promise with others we must lead by example. We must take risks.

We must risk having our view challenged, risk being seen as out of touch, and even clueless. We might even have to risk being ridiculed, berated, and even abused. We must risk losing in the short term.

Risk takers know what we stand for and we stand. We accept what others say as a view and don't take personally anything someone else says that may seem derogatory.

Risk takers know that we are responsible for our own intentions, feelings, thoughts, and actions. We are not responsible for other people's intentions, feelings, thoughts, and actions. And we are only affected by them when we choose to be.

Risk takers know that short term pain often leads to long term gain, for all.

As I have shared previously, we live in three worlds. The world in here (my view), the world out there (your view) and the world we share (our view). In the scheme of things, focusing only on the world we share really matters, when it comes to collaboration, because from shared view comes a co-promise to stand together and take action for the common good.

Risk takers are innovators more than problem solvers. When we solve problems, it almost always means a return to what is normal or the status quo.

When we innovate on the other hand, we change what's normal.

Are you are risk taker?

One sign that you are, or are not, is whether or not you are doing what you love in the service of people who love what you do.

Other signs that you are a risk taker are your willingness to:

✓ speak out against injustice.
✓ go against the flow when you see a possible better way forward for all.
✓ speak up even when no one else does.
✓ say what you mean and mean what you say even when it is uncomfortable.
✓ put your insights and ideas forward not worrying about how they will be received.
✓ work hard on relationships (which also requires risk) knowing that outcomes are a consequence of processes.

Possibility Actions:

Take time out to review your performance in the past six months and answer the following questions:

How many times did you compromise where the result was a win/lose, a lose/win, or a lose/lose?

How many times did you avoid compromise and achieve a co-promise and the result was win/win?

What lessons can you take away from your compromises and your co-promises that you can apply next time you have the choice that will change what's normal, lead you to more win/win, and perhaps even a win for a wider group of people and/or our planet?

Do your work.

Differentiate: Sparkenations 15 - 18

I have worked with many organisations to help them differentiate themselves.

One suggestion I always make is: *"Let's get as many people as we can being their true selves."* I get blank looks on most occasions.

I then discuss with my client that differentiation is primarily about their people doing what their competitors' people don't do, or at very least inspiring their people to do what others do, only differently, better, or more uniquely.

I then ask my client to imagine what would happen to their business if just a few more people really stood up and brought their best, one-of-a-kind selves to their work on a consistent basis. The answer I always get is *"There would be a significant difference to our results for the better."*

To differentiate ourselves we firstly need to bring our best to everything we do. This is explored in Sparkenation 15.

From there we need to focus on giving, following proven processes, and competing only with the person we looked at in the mirror this morning. These are Sparkenations 16, 17, and 18.

Sparkenation 15.
The toughest yet
most rewarding journey

Normal

Most of us only hear what we want to hear.

Changing What's Normal

There is paradox to all aspects of life and even though most of the feedback we get we didn't ask for, we must not fail to hear it because some feedback can be life-changing. And even with *feedforward* we may not want to hear it, yet we must still hear.

In my very early days of speaking professionally I invited people to a three hour preview workshop of my work in my home city. I had been a highly successful corporate executive and therefore thought I had plenty of value to share with business people.

At the half way break an elderly gentleman, who I hadn't previously met, came to me and asked if he could see me privately.

We went over to a corner of the room and he said *"You are obviously a very smart young man."*
"Thank you", I said.
He then said *"It's a bloody shame you are not showing it!"*

He then pleaded with me to go back in and in the second half speak from my heart and not my head. *"Tell us some passionate stories from your life"*, he told me.

I was quite thrown by this encounter and I don't remember much of the second half of my workshop. I do know that this was a defining moment in my career and a turning point of my business. Not long after this encounter I did a session with legendary speaking coach David Griggs. In those days David's studio was an old court house that still had all the court furniture in place.

Sitting at a table David asked me to present my best material. My presentation space was the section between the gallery and the dock and, although intimidated, I squared my shoulders, took a deep breath and launched into my best work.

I lasted a few minutes when David put up his hand indicating for me to stop. I was quite miffed thinking I had 45 minutes to speak. He then sat me down and proceeded to tell me that he saw many of my heroes in my presentation, which I took as a compliment until he said: *"I didn't see much of Ian Berry however."*

I was quite shocked, yet I was also beginning to get it. Another defining moment.

Success in life is firstly about being ourselves, that one-of-a-kind that each of us is. It is about recognising our specialness.

This is easier said than done. It has taken me, and many people I know, a lot of personal work to become comfortable in our own skins. And it is a never-ending and sometimes painful journey. In the quest to find myself I have lost friends and business. I have also gained new friends, respect, and most importantly, self respect.

When I stand with an audience today I can tell you that what you see is what you get and that I share stories from my heart.

Possibility Action:

Really get to know yourself, warts and all, and decide to bring everything you are to everything you do.

A simple way to take action on this sparkenation is to take a sheet of paper and divide it into two columns. In one column write down all of the things you currently celebrate as valuable about your life. In the other column write down all the things that could be better in your life. Then each week add something to the 'celebrations' column, and eliminate something from the 'could be better' column.

"Be yourself; everyone else is already taken."
Oscar Wilde

Do your work.

Sparkenation 16.
Wanting and getting
and having and giving

Normal

It has been said that there are two broad kinds of people in the world - givers and takers.

The givers ask *"what's in me for you?"*

The takers ask *"what's in it for me?"*

Takers currently rule the world.

Changing What's Normal

I think we are all givers and takers.

Intention is what differentiates.

I meet lots of people who have been takers all their lives. They are generally very unhappy people. They want and get the so called finer things of life and yet the most precious gift of all - happiness - alludes them.

I also meet lots of people who have been givers all their lives. Givers of all they have. Many don't have the finer things of life and yet they have a happiness that is inspiring.

My attitude to life is to first be grateful. I have learned that when we are grateful for what we've got, we can have more of what we want, usually as a consequence of giving of what we have.

My focus is to give of all I've got without attachment to getting back. The great paradox is that giving with such intent means we end up getting back a thousand-fold and often from people we haven't yet given to.

What intentions drive you?

We can want and get. It seems to me, however, that the most precious things in life come to us by giving of what we have without attachment to getting back.

Another way of looking at this paradox is the concept of free and fee. I make my living giving tailored talks that stir hearts, shift thinking, and inspire people to step-up their achievements; providing meaningful and measurable mentoring; and conducting 'changing what's normal' programs for organisations or leadership development programs for people who lead such programs.

I also give away a ton of resources for free here: www.ianberry.biz/courses-and-resources/

The paradox for me is that the more I give away, the more valuable buyers see my services that require a fee.

Possibility Actions:

The givers ask *"what's in me for you?"*

The takers ask *"what's in it for me?"*

What changes could you take or make in your life to be more of a giver? Make a list.

I recommend you read an excellent book called *The Go-Giver* by Bob Burg and John David Mann, Portfolio/Penguin Group 2007.

The following are five laws from Bob and John. The living of these laws are a tremendous help to me in changing what's normal.

The Law of Value

Your true worth is determined by how much more you give in value than you take in payment.

The Law of Compensation

Your income is determined by how many people you serve and how well you serve them.

The Law of influence

Your influence is determined by how abundantly you place other people's interest first.

The Law of Authenticity

The most valuable gift you have to offer is yourself.

The Law of Receptivity

The key to effective giving is to stay open to receiving.

Do your work.

Sparkenation 17.
Grandpa's Legacy and a key law
for living a good life

Normal

Most people expect the best outcomes and yet are unwilling to do the work which will mean the desired outcomes happen as a consequence.

Changing What's Normal

My Grandfather, Frederick Sherriff, died when I was 14. I loved Pa. He was a big man with a big heart who had a tremendous influence on everyone who met him.

One day Pa summoned me to his garden. Originally a farmer, Pa loved his garden with a passion.

As we squatted down amongst his flowers he said to me, *"I want to share with you the most important thing I have ever learned. Life is just like the farm. We must discover the fertile ground, plough it, seed it, nurture it and then, more often than not, we will reap a harvest."*

As he pulled a flower and sniffed its scent Pa said *"So many people want to reap the harvest life is, but they are not prepared to find the fertile ground, plough it, seed it, and nurture it."*

I have met so many people in my life, and I have to admit I have been one myself, who expect the harvest but are not prepared to find the fertile ground and do the ploughing, seeding, and nurturing.

Grandpa died about two weeks after our conversation. His legacy lives on. I have spent a great deal of my life endeavouring to understand and apply Grandpa's wisdom.

Grandpa believed we reap what we sow. Today we say, *"what goes around comes around"* or *"we get what we give"*. However we say it, this changeless law of life is a key to us living the significant life we were all born to live.

Grandpa's legacy will help us on several occasions throughout this book.

The law of the farm is a great example from many laws of nature about how things work. It shows us that there is a process or a sequence to changing what's normal.

The fertile ground is the starting place. It is where we begin. Things do grow in infertile ground of course. However, the best chance for something to grow is in fertile ground.

In the world in here (our world) the starting place, the fertile ground, is intention or purpose. In the world we share, the starting place, the fertile ground, is in how we make contact with people.

The second sequential step for the farmer is ploughing the ground, getting it ready for planting seeds. In the world in here, this step is about engaging our emotions. We are unlikely to make further progress if we are not engaged emotionally. In the world we share, this step is about making emotional connection with other people.

Once the ground is ready the farmer plants the seeds. In the world in here, this third step is about engaging our thoughts.

Doing so means we have moved from intent to emotionally engaged, to carrying the change we want to make in our minds. In the world we share, this third step is about finding common ground with an individual or group that we have already built some kind of relationship with, through emotional connection and good contact.

No farmer worth his/her salt just leaves the seeds planted to grow on their own.   Nurturing is required by watering, weeding, fertilizing and a host of other actions, in order to give the seeds the best chance to grow.   In the world in here, we can have the right intention, be emotionally engaged, and be thinking right, however, until we take action nothing is going to change in the real world.   In the world we share, this fourth step is all about demonstrating and receiving commitment through real actions that are moving us further to whatever it is we have agreed to do together.

More often than not, when a farmer finds fertile ground, ploughs it, plants seeds and nurtures their growth, a harvest is the result. Sure, things happen which are outside of the farmer's control, like floods and fires, however, the point is that the farmer has done everything within his/her power to produce a great crop.

When we align our intentions, feelings, thoughts, and take action we have done everything within our power to change what's normal.

When we make the right kind of contact with other people, make emotional connection with them, find common ground, and demonstrate commitment we have done everything in our power to enhance the relationship.

Possibility Actions:

What underlying philosophies guide your life?

In what areas of your life could you better live your philosophies?

What proven processes do you follow that will, within the spheres of your influence, guarantee the outcomes you want?

Make a list of actions about how you could better live your philosophies and follow proven processes. Then get about doing.

Do your work.

Sparkenation 18.
Compete with Yourself

Normal

Most people are waiting for other people to change before they will consider changing.

Changing What's Normal

John F. Kennedy is credited as saying:

"I thought someone should do something, and then I realised, I was someone."

We cannot change anyone except ourselves.

I have met many leaders who thought they could change other people.   Living with such an intention leads to nothing but frustration and ineffectiveness, and eventually self-destruction.

When we focus on changing ourselves, however, we inspire others to make their own changes.

Our only real competitor is the person we looked at in the mirror this morning.   Our key quest in life is to take responsibility for that someone.

The **fertile ground** for competing with ourselves is **intention or purpose.**
ploughing is to do with **feelings,**
seeding with **thoughts,**
nurturing with **behaviour** and the
harvest is the outcome of the these four.

One follows the other like night follows day. If we want a different/better harvest in our lives, and I believe most of us do, we must change/modify our behaviour.

However, changing/modifying our behaviour, if the new behaviour is to become a habit, requires us to first change/modify our thinking, our feelings, and our intention.

Ever wondered why most training programs fail to result in changes for the better?

It is because people return to work with the same intentions, feelings, and thoughts that they had before they undertook the training!

Possibility Action:

In the online learning vault that is a companion to this book there is an exercise, 'Compete with yourself', that you can undertake anytime you wish to change or modify your intentions, feelings, thoughts, and behaviours, and as a consequence achieve better outcomes in your life.

You can access it at www.changingwhatsnormal.com/vault/

Do your work.

Deliver: Sparkenations 19 - 23

I once worked with a colleague whose favourite phrase (unbeknown's to him) was *"good enough"*. He would get to a certain point with a task, and even in his relationships, and feel that *"that will do, it's enough to get by, it will be passable"*.

Mediocrity has no place in changing what's normal, indeed it is one of the maladies we want to eliminate.

To really deliver our best on a consistent basis means:

✓ Never just show up.

✓ Maintaining an attitude of gratitude regardless of what is happening in our lives.

✓ Being fully alive, which I define as being spiritually alive, emotionally healthy, mentally alert, physically active, and universally aware.

✓ Making ourselves indispensable.

✓ Accepting and managing the fact that there is some pain in being an exception, and that there is also a great deal of pleasure.

Sparkenation 19.
Just showing up isn't enough

Normal

I came across the following at Persistence Unlimited.

> *"80 percent of success is just showing up."*
> Woody Allen

> *"I often think about that quotation. It may sound easy to shrug off, but not if you look a little deeper. It doesn't just mean show up for job interviews or to work for an 80% increase in success. Showing up also means ... starting.*
>
> *For instance, did you show up at the gym today? Just showing up means you're 80% of the way to a good workout. The hard part of fighting yourself to get dressed in workout gear, dealing with traffic and the worry about pain you might experience is over. Now all that is left is to just do the workout. Pretty simple, huh? Even a child could do it.*
>
> *Same thing with opportunity. It's easier to make significant progress on a project if you simply show up to do it. Candidly, one of my hardest tasks of the day is 'showing up' for development Visual Studio. It seems simple enough ... just double click on an icon. But if I think too much about the seemingly 10,000 things I have to do once I launch it, I am much more likely to 'accidentally' launch my web browser or fiddle with e-mail.*

But once I'm in there, the work is typically easy and fun.   Some days I can knock out more tasks than I planned. And I feel like a success at the end of the day.

You can be or do whatever you want just by showing up. If you want to be an author, show up to write your manuscript every day, show up to writing classes, show up to phone calls to editors. Doesn't it make sense that someone who arrives at the door of opportunity has more success than someone just sitting at home?
So increase your chances by 80%. Show Up!"

Changing What's Normal

I reflected on this piece of advice a lot and it played a critical part in me deciding on my mantra to *"show up joyful."*

This has made an incredible difference to my life and work. I agree showing up is a key to being successful.   I am firm, however, that the attitude we bring to our showing up, and what we actually deliver, is the real key.

Possibility Action:

How are you showing up?

What changes could you make so that you showing up in ways that mean you are bringing everything you are to everything you do?

Be the changes you decide to make.

Do your work.

Sparkenation 20.
Have an attitude of gratitude

Normal

Most people lack being in gratitude for where their life is right now and instead have a roving eye on how their life could be better.

Changing What's Normal

I was born with a small birthmark on the inside of my right knee. In my youth I often scratched it to the point of bleeding whilst playing football. I would get it bandaged and play on.

It ended up becoming a malignant melanoma which was removed in my 21st year.   The doctor who performed this minor surgery told me nothing of the possible dangers of a malignant melanoma.

A few years later I ended up with another melanoma and required major surgery. At that time, only 1 in 5 people survived the kind of secondary melanoma that I had.

The doctor who performed this second surgery was not the same doctor who had performed the first surgery, thankfully!

His advice in helping me to prepare for the five-hour operation surprised me to say the least. He said *"The secret to getting well is to have an attitude of gratitude."*

I had never heard the expression before nor the followup remark from my doctor who said: *"When we are grateful for what we've got, we can have more of what we want."*

In the days before my operation I would stand several times a day in front of a mirror and say, *"I have an attitude of gratitude."*

I didn't believe what I was saying at first, of course. However, this affirmation soon became a part of my daily life and still is today.
Are you grateful for every aspect of your life right now?

Being grateful changed what was normal for me.

Three years after this second surgery I was faced with a third tumour and was given only 90 days to live. I am in no doubt whatsoever that my habit of being grateful was a key to my survival.

To be grateful every day, regardless of our circumstances, is a key step to changing what's normal and to co-creating the new world that is waiting to be born.

This sounds simple right? Simple rarely means easy. Despite my life experience I still find that there are times when I am not grateful for what I've got and a lot of personal work is required to get back on track. All change is personal first.

Possibility Actions:

Please download 12 ways to maintain an attitude of gratitude from the vault www.changingwhatsnormal.com/vault/ and pin it/ paste it, whatever, somewhere that you will see it everyday, until you are living the 12 and when you slip out of gratitude get the 12 back in your focus straight away.

Read the book *The Power of Now* by Eckhart Tolle.
Do your work.

Sparkenation 21.
A human being fully alive

Normal

Most people are barely awake and instead live their lives on auotmatic pilot, not aware of the infinite possibilities which are available to human beings who are fully alive.

Changing What's Normal

When I was a boy my father often used to say that a key to living a good life was to be **spiritually alive, mentally alert,** and **physically active**.

Over time I added **emotionally healthy** and **universally aware** and thereby created what I call the five faces of a human being fully alive.

For me, being spiritually alive is the **fertile ground** of living a good life. When we are **spiritually alive we feel valued.** When we feel valued we are best able to capitalise on our unique gifts/ talents in the service of others, show our true character, and be committed, courageous, honest, and to live with integrity.

For me being emotionally healthy is the **ploughing.** When we are **emotionally healthy we feel at peace.** When we feel at peace we are able to be caring, joyful, kind, open, patient, passionate. Feeling at peace is sometimes hard work. Yet the work ends in joy.

For me being mentally alert is the **seeding.** When we are **mentally alert** we are **feeling clear.**

When we are feeling clear we are able to have an *"attitude of gratitude"*, to visualise, and to be focused, insightful, inspired, all of which are key to doing things right for us and doing the right thing by others.

For me being physically active is the **nurturing.** When we are **physically active** (regardless of our physical capabilities, which differ for us all of course) we are **feeling well.** When we feel well we are fit and able to be accountable, competent, energetic, productive, and innovative.

For me being universally aware is key to creating a **harvest.**

When we are **universally aware** we **feel connected.** When we feel connected we are able to maximise the high value and mutual reward of one-degree relationships, and active social networks. We are awake, conscious, enlightened and can live the unchanging laws of life (such as the law of the farm) to the full and, in doing so, achieve whatever we dream we can.

Be (spiritually alive), **Feel** (emotionally healthy), **See** (mentally alert), **Do** (physically active) and you can **Have** (universally aware) anything you want and yet not harm the planet or another person in the process.

Possibility Action:

Are you a human being fully alive?

Please use the diagram on the next pages as a check on your state of being and then change what's normal in any areas where you feel you are out of alignment.

Laws we get what we give what goes around comes around karma the law of the farm	States of Being	Personal Practice compete with yourself
1. Fertile Ground **Be/Is**	**Spiritually alive** feeling valued appreciate self; appreciate others; self respect; respect for others	**Intention** Mine is to make a difference; inspire others to make a difference. What's yours?
2. Ploughing **Feel**	**Emotionally healthy** feeling at peace passionate	**Feelings** I am appreciative, joyful, allowing. How are you?
3. Seeding **See**	**Mentally alert** feeling clear	**Thoughts** Mine are positive and productive. How are yours?

Laws we get what we give what goes around comes around karma the law of the farm	States of Being	Personal Practice compete with yourself
4. Nurturing **Do**	**Physically active** feeling well being accountable; being a role model	**Behaviours** My best are: collaborative; open; passionate; committed; inspirational. What are your best behaviours?
5. Harvest **Know/Have**	**Universally aware** feeling connected family, friends, business partners, networks, advocates, centres of influence	**Outcomes** Mine are: made a difference, have inspired others to have made a difference, achieved personal goals, helped others to achieve their goals. Yours are?

Do your work.

Sparkenation 22.
Being indispensable

Normal

We are inspired by people who really make a difference and yet not inspired enough to make a difference ourselves. Instead most of us live ordinary lives in quiet discontent.

Changing What's Normal

"You must be the change you want to see in the world" as Gandhi suggested long ago. Such change is a personal journey first and then it continues in our homes and in our neighbourhoods and local communities, our organisations, and then the rest of the world.

Possibility actions:

Read Seth Godin's landmark book *Linchpin* about how to be indispensable. I get Seth's blog every day. I think *Linchpin* is one of his best works. It helped me to get really clear on who is indispensable in my life and why, and how I can be better in being indispensable in the lives of others.

Who is indispensable in your life?

Have you shown appreciation to them this week?

Who are you indispensable to?

Read Peter Sheahan's *Making $#IT Happen* as well.

We all have great ideas.   The issue for most of us is turning our ideas into great results.   I have never read a better book on this subject than Peter's.   It helped me get really clear on who and what I need to focus on to really make the difference I was born to make in my world.

Read *Thought Leaders - how to capture, package and deliver your ideas for greater commercial success* by Matt Church with Scott Stein and Michael Henderson.

I don't know anyone better than Matt at turning ideas into action.

What is happening with your ideas? Are they in your head? Are they in your heart?   Or are they out in the world making a difference?

Do your work.

Sparkenation 23.
The pleasure and pain
of being an exception

Normal

Most people prefer to blend in rather than stand out.

Changing What's Normal

Alan Weiss, one of my heroes, puts out a memo every Monday morning USA time. It is a pithy thought from him and a quote from someone else.

A recent memo from Alan contained this quote:
"How glorious it is -- and also how painful -- to be an exception."
Alfred de Musset

This is the classic paradox of personal change and perhaps why many people avoid changing; it is pleasurable and it can also be painful. Are you up for it?

Possibility Action:

To really stimulate your thinking at the start of every week subscribe to Alan Weiss' Monday Morning Memo and renew your commitment to being an exception at the start of every week.

Do your work.

Action 2:
Change Your Relationships.

**Relationship change follows
personal change.
Sparkenations 24 - 28**

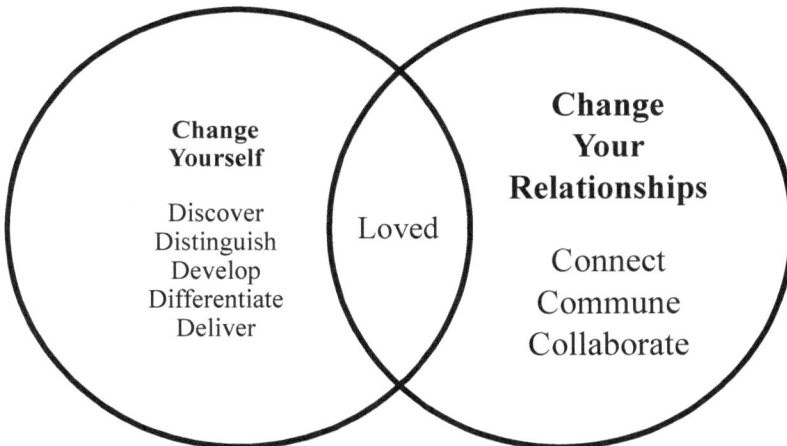

**Change
Yourself**

Discover
Distinguish
Develop
Differentiate
Deliver

Loved

**Change
Your
Relationships**

Connect
Commune
Collaborate

Connect, Commune, Collaborate
Sparkenations 24 - 28

When we change what's normal ourselves and within our relationships we end up being loved.

I vowed in May of 2007 I would no longer go to networking functions. I had grown very tired of going to events full of self-promoters with no genuine interest in other people. There had to be a better way.

It took some time, energy, and effort, however, through building relationships of high value and mutual reward, both online and in person, I slowly began to not need to go to the typical networking event. And then my friend and colleague, Kwai Yu, the Founder and CEO of Leaders Cafe, introduced me to Melissa Giovagnoli, the Founder of Networlding, a 21st century way to build and grow great relationships. I was shocked to discover through networlding that many of the relationships I was pursuing were with people I didn't really have a values match with and therefore communing and collaborating successfully was not possible.

Embracing networlding as outlined in Sparkenation 24 has changed what's normal in my life and my relationships both personal and professional, so much so that this is the shortest section in this book because I believe only 5 actions really matter. These are:

- ✓ Networlding
- ✓ Being a hero in our own home first
- ✓ Life/work harmony
- ✓ Belonging to tribes
- ✓ Only collaborating with people when you have achieved a shared view

Sparkenation 24.
Networking with purpose
- introducing Networlding

Normal

Networking is seen as a necessary evil by most people and is undertaken grudgingly because it is seen as a 'have to do', particularly by business people, in order to stay in touch and be seen and to possibly extend or uncover business opportunities.

Changing What's Normal

Two years ago I was introduced to the concept of Networlding and I participated in a webinar presented by founder Melissa Giovagnoli. I was immediately taken by the differences between traditional networking and networlding and I soon began to practice them. The results astounded me. So much so that I became the Ambassador to Australia for Networlding and earlier this year I presented the first classes in Australia to inspire other people to engage in the practice.

Networking	Networlding
Transactional	Transformational
Goal based	Values based
Undisciplined effort	Leveraged effort
Temporary	Long term
Often one-sided	Mutually beneficial
Haphazard	Strategic
Fragmented	Systematic
Superficial	Authentic
Opportunity specific	Opportunity expansive
Two dimensional	Multi-dimensional
Push	Pull

Networlding is not about the number of connections you have on LinkedIn, the number of followers you have on Twitter, or the legion of fans you have Facebook, nor the size of your business card collection – **it is about the quality of the connections** you have and develop.

Networlding is a powerful concept to embrace because it involves ensuring a values match with people before you pursue a business relationship; and once such a values match is confirmed, relationships are only pursued with people who meet the following criteria:

1. *Have a wide variety of connections*
2. *Are observant of people and environment*
3. *Have a talent for staying in touch*
4. *Are outwardly focused*
5. *Are sensitive to other's needs*
6. *Have access to different information*
7. *Have a natural talent for helping*
8. *Are focused on diversity*
9. *Are spiritually, intellectually, and emotionally balanced*
10. *Are influencers to a broad base*

The Tipping Point by Malcolm Gladwell is one of my favourite books about change and how change can happen quickly. Malcolm refers to three kinds of people who are critical to the spreading of a story, an idea, anything; *"Mavens, Connectors, and Salespeople."*

Mavens are people in the know and who are across the details of things.

Connectors are people with a special gift for bringing people together and are also gifted at spreading the word.

Salespeople are people who are persuaders, influencers, and inspirers.

How many *Mavens, Connectors, and Salespeople* do you know?

And more importantly how many people know you as a *Maven, Connector, or Salesperson,* or all three?

After reading *The Tipping Point,* when it first came out, I immediately caste a critical eye over all my connections to see how many of these kinds of people I knew and began to focus on pursuing relationships of mutual reward with such people. I also closely reviewed all my business relationships where I thought people would see me as *Maven, Connector, Salesperson,* or all three, and began to strengthen my ties with these people.

When I first embraced Networlding I was shocked that with many of the *Mavens, Connectors, and Salespeople* I knew, and with many people who knew me as having the skills, there wasn't a values match, and when there was, very few people met the 10 criteria stated on the previous page.

Since then I have begun to build relationships of mutual reward with vastly different people to those I had in the past and the results have taken my breath away.

Possibility actions:

As I write there are Networlding Circles in Australia, United Kingdom, and United States of America. Melissa is very keen to expand these to everywhere. Get in touch with Melissa.

At very least buy Melissa's books and learn to Networld yourself.

There are links about Networlding in the vault
www.changingwhatsnormal.com/vault/

You will be amazed at how Networlding will help you to change what's normal.

Do your work.

Sparkenation 25.
Be a hero in your own home first

Normal

There is conflict for most people between work and home life and never the twain shall meet and one is seen as a means for success in the other.

Changing What's Normal

The first place we must collaborate in is own own homes.

At the peak of my corporate career in 1989 when I was working over 100 hours and mostly 7 days a week, I decided on one particular day, to arrive home early. I had picked up a new company car on this particular day, the first I had ever driven with electric windows.

On the way home, as I played with the new windows, I began to reflect on my life. It's fair to say that, by the time I arrived home, I had a big head thinking how well I had done from poor beginnings and on how well I was providing for my wife and two children.

With a beaming smile, I got out of my new shining car to greet my wife who was standing at the top of the stairs. Right off the bat she said *"We need to talk!"* Now I'm sure that all you male readers will realise how ominous this was!

She then said *"Your children do not know who their father is."* and after a long pause she said *"I'm starting to wonder as well."*

You see, I was a hero in my own mind yet not in the hearts and minds of the people who mattered the most to me.

A few days later my daughter came into my study and asked *"Hey Dad, can I get a video?"*
I will never forget the look on her face when I said: *"Yes. Let's go."* Previously I would have told her to get lost or said *"Can't you see I'm busy!"*

The videos we rented that day were her choice, *Anne of Green Gables* - in two parts!

She was even more surprised when I sat on the couch to watch them with her.

At a certain point in the first part I began to cry. This was the first time my daughter had ever seen me cry. I was raised with the belief that real men don't cry and had hidden my emotions until that day. Real men do cry.

I changed what was normal for me from that day forward and it has made an incredible difference to the lives of my family, and many other people, as I have shared this experience worldwide.

> ***It's not what the world holds for you.***
> ***It is what you bring to it.***
> Anne of Green Gables

Possibility Action:

In the online learning vault at www.changingwhatsnormal.com/vault/ there is an exercise you can undertake, anytime, to see how much of a hero you are in your own home. The exercise is not for the faint hearted yet it is worth maximum effort.
Do your work.

Sparkenation 26.
Life/work balance is nonsense

Normal

I hear a lot of talk about life/work balance and I think most of it is nonsense.

The word balance for me implies equal. My personal and business life are not equal or in balance and are never likely to be, and neither are yours.

Changing What's Normal

I use the word harmony because life/work harmony is what is possible.

Our personal and business lives can be in harmony with one another. That is, they can work together as a part of the symphony of the whole of our lives.

Here are my 11 laws of life/work harmony. I trust they will help you live a more harmonious life.

1. The Law of Harmony

There are always at least two sides to every story.
Opposites attract.

Possibility Actions: Always think both/and, rather than either/or; accept the good with the bad; appreciate pleasure, gain from pain; focus on the positive, learn from the negative; and you will soon begin to find harmony in your life.

2. The Law of Possibility

The opportunities life offers us are endless. There are no limits, except those we place on ourselves. There is nothing we cannot achieve.

Possibility Action: When you find yourself in any situation that seems hopeless, rather than focusing on what is, focus on what's possible.

3. The Law of Personal Responsibility

No one else can make us feel or think glad, sad, bad or mad. How we feel and think are choices we make.

Possibility Actions: We must own our feelings and thoughts and not get tangled in other people's feelings and thoughts. We must let go of attachment to what other people feel and think. Soon we eliminate guilt and worry; two of life's most useless and most debilitating emotions.

4. The Law of Attraction

Success is not something we attain, rather it's something we attract.

Possibility Actions: Commit to life-long learning; focus on insight more than information and wisdom more than knowledge. The more we become who we are capable of becoming the more we attract success.

5. The Law of the Farm

You find fertile ground, plough it, seed it, and nurture it, and, more often than not, you reap a harvest. We get what we give. What goes around comes around. These are modern ways of describing an old adage; we reap what we sow.

Possibility Actions: The message of this law is that we must focus on proven processes and detach from outcomes. If we are taking the right action, results take care of themselves.

6. The Law of Relationships

We gravitate to those we like, know and trust.

Possibility Actions: Establish shared values with family, friends and work colleagues, and agree on how they will be lived. Have shared goals and agree on the key strategies to achieve them. Practice non-judgment. Give genuine attention to others. Before you know it, your relationships will be stronger and the great door of opportunity will open more often.

7. The Law of Service

Giving without attachment to getting back creates one of life's great paradoxes; we get more back.

Possibility Actions: Fully understand what others need and provide it. Go the extra mile by adding value to every transaction and interaction. Co-create wow experiences at work, home and play. Before long, others will be serving you in ways beyond your wildest expectations.

8. The Law of Confidence

Having confidence is to maintain positive inner and outer images of ourselves and display them.

Possibility Actions: Demonstrate openness to learning. Be assertive without believing your way is the only way. Believe in yourself. Believe in others. Speak and communicate from your heart and confidence will rarely get mistaken for arrogance.

9. The Law of Actual Communication

Not all talk is communication. We often talk just for the joy of it. To actually communicate is to agree on some course of action even if it is to agree to disagree.

Possibility Actions: To communicate better, speak with a specific goal in mind and listen simply to understand. When speaking and listening, ask for feedback to ensure message effectiveness. You will most likely find that you will speak less and listen more. The result is to eventually eliminate misunderstanding, one of the great causes of negative stress.

10. The Law of Adaptability

I heard a great saying one time *"better to adapt than be a sitting duck and get run over."*

Possibility Actions: Our willingness to adapt, be flexible, and go with the flow are keys to a negative-stress free life. A key seems to be to realise, *"it is not what happens to you, it's what you do about it"* (thank you W. Mitchell). Take responsibility for your responses to life and life will respond to you.

11. The Law of Synchronicity/Interconnectedness

Everything is connected, in some way, to everything else.

Possibility Actions: Seek coincidence, follow your heart, do what you love.

Have a personal sustainability plan (thank you Adam Werbach for the idea from his book *Strategies for Sustainability*) i.e. do what you can personally do for the good of people and our planet. Imagine if everyone did this.
We would have universal harmony.

Do your work.

Sparkenation 27.
The triumph of tribes

Normal

Most people are trying to hang out in too many places, particularly now with the explosion that is social media/social networking, and often for the wrong reasons. The result is a drop off in focus, time wasting, and in the end a significant reduction in productivity.

Engaging in social media/social networking online without a clear intention and a strategy is perhaps the greatest example of 'jumping on the bandwagon' in history.

Changing What's Normal

My first serious foray into social media/social networking began with the posting of my first blog in May 2007. I didn't really know then why I was blogging. I just felt I should because of what a lot of people I respected were saying.

When the number of visits to my web site soon quadrupled, I began to spend a lot of time and energy online endeavouring to work out what it all meant for me.

I joined more than 100 social networking sites including LinkedIn, Facebook, and ecademy. I also explored YouTube and a zillion other places. I became totally consumed and incredibly unproductive over several months. One day I threw up my hands in total frustration and shouted *"What am I doing?"* It then dawned on me that I was focusing on what I could possibly get, rather than what I could give, and I had no idea of where I was, where I was going, why I was doing all this 'work', and I had no strategy.

I had allowed myself to become sucked in and was doing what pretty much everyone else was doing - self-promotion. I took time out and came to my senses.

After much soul-searching I left most of the social media/social networking sites I was playing in, having decided that, for me, most were full of self-promoters engaged in talk fests and grandstanding.

At that time (my pre-Networlding days) I was providing online learning resources for many of my clients as part of a package for my tailored talks, change programs, and 1:1 mentoring. I realised there was a common theme amongst many of my clients, that of wanting to make a difference.

In November 2008 I founded the *differencemakers community* as a private forum to engage in ongoing dialogue with my clients who had a passion for making a difference and to provide a central place where these folk could gain easy access to my digital resources.

After testing and adjustments I opened up *differencemakers* to the world in February 2009. In the same week I joined the Leaders Cafe group on LinkedIn, believing it to be a group I could make a valued contribution to.   Later that week I was working in Birmingham in the United Kingdom and noticed Kwai Yu, the founder of the Leaders Cafe group on LindedIn, lived near by. I sent Kwai an email asking if he would like to meet.   At considerable inconvenience to him, Kwai came to meet me. It was as though we had known each other all of our lives and today we have a wonderful relationship of high value and mutual reward.

Around this time I read Seth Godin's wonderful book, *Tribes*, which confirmed that social media/social networking for me was about:

✓ giving where I could provide real value.
✓ building relationships with people with whom I have a shared interest.
✓ connecting people of like heart and mind together.
✓ making it simple for people of like heart and mind to connect with one another.
✓ attracting the people with whom I could collaborate to make a difference and increase the scale of differencemaking in the world.
✓ increasing the speed at which I could inspire and influence people to make a difference.
✓ building real world relationships over time that would be of high value and mutual reward.

Possibility actions:

Check out Leaders Cafe on LinkedIn.

Check out the many groups that Kwai and my friends have co-created in the Manchester area of the United Kingdom, MojoLife, Speakeasy, and Linchpin Academy. Kwai, Sara, Andrew, and Lily, and the many others involved, are wonderful role models of how social media/social networking can be used effectively to co-create online and real world tribes (communities) that change what's normal.

Links to the work of these wonderful folk are in the vault.
www.changingwhatsnormal.com/vault/

Decide the following:

Why are you engaged in social media/social networking?

Where are you going with social media/social networking?

What is your strategy to get where you're going with social media/social networking?

There will be many sparkenations in the section on organisational change that follows that will help you to answer these questions.

Be sure of this: engagement that is right for you in social media/ social networking will play a key role in your changing of what's normal.

The power of people using social media to connect with one another for a common cause, and then to take action together, was one of the sparkenations that brought about the beginnings of changing what's normal in Egypt, Libya, and other places in 2011. What could you do?

Do your work.

Sparkenation 28.
Only collaborate with people when you have achieved a shared view

Normal

"No man is an island, entire of itself."   Yet this is what most people feel and think.

Changing What's Normal

The **fertile ground** for collaborating with others is **contact**.
Ploughing is to do with **connection,**
seeding with **common ground,**
nurturing with **commitment** and the
harvest is the continuity of the relationship/s.

One follows the other like night follows day. If we want different/better relationships in our lives, and I believe most of us do, we must change/modify our commitment to the person or people we want a better relationship with.

Changing/modifying our commitment, if the new kind of commitment is to become a habit, requires us to first change/modify our contact, our connection, and our ability and willingness to discover common ground with the person or people.

7 steps to success collaboration

A few times in my life I have felt let down by, what I perceived, was a betrayal by others of perceived agreements to do certain things.

The last time this happened I allowed myself to feel hurt for many months. The positive consequence was that I developed a process for reaching agreement with others.   I trust you will find it valuable in making your collaborations successful.

Remember there are three worlds: The one in here - that's my world; the one out there - that's your world; and the one that is vital when it comes to collaboration - the world we share. We are looking to collaborate only with people with whom we can reach shared views.

I find that there are three main reasons for human conflict:

1. disagreement about the goal/s, objective/s, or aim/s.
2. disagreement about how the goal/s, objective/s, or aim/s will be achieved.
3. assumption of agreement in 1. and/or 2., and a negative response when such assumptions result in perceived betrayal.

Seven special steps to successful collaboration

1. Establish that there is agreement concerning the goal/s, objective/s, or aim/s.   Don't move on until you are absolutely certain there is agreement.
2. State what you can and will do to achieve the goal/s, objective/s, or aim/s.
3. Ask the other person or people involved to state what they can and will do to achieve the goal/s, objective/s, or aim/s.
4. State what you feel are the milestones or measurements that will indicate that you are on on track to achieve what you say you will in 2.
5. Ask the other person or people involved to state what they feel are the milestones or measurements that will indicate

that they are on on track to achieve what they say they will in 3.

6. Agree on the dates and times that you will be in touch with each other to discuss progress and celebrate achievements.

7. Confirm in writing via email or letter your agreements in 2. through 6. and ask for a confirmation response from the other person or people involved.

Possibility Action:

In the online learning vault there is an exercise you can undertake anytime you wish to improve a relationship.
Look for 'Collaborate'.

You can access it at www.changingwhatsnormal.com/vault/

Begin straight away. Don't put this off. Choose a relationship that you would like to be better.

Do your work.

Action 3:
Change your organisation.

**The most powerful organisational
change follows relationships and
personal change.
Sparkenations 29 - 58**

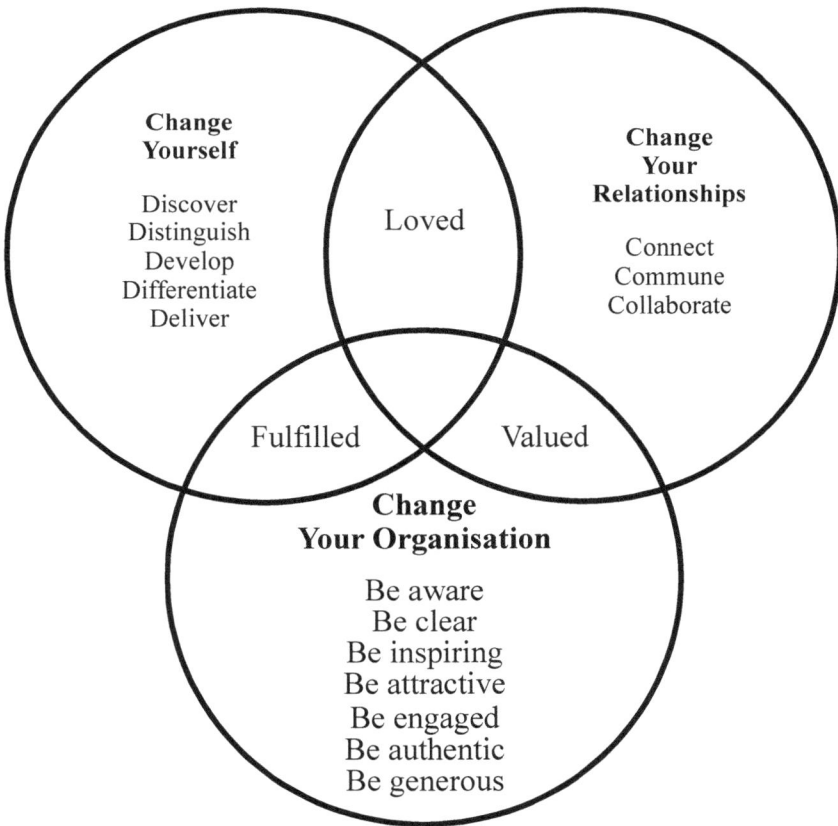

**Change
Yourself**

Discover
Distinguish
Develop
Differentiate
Deliver

Loved

**Change
Your
Relationships**

Connect
Commune
Collaborate

Fulfilled

Valued

**Change
Your Organisation**

Be aware
Be clear
Be inspiring
Be attractive
Be engaged
Be authentic
Be generous

Be aware. Sparkenations 29 - 31

Most people think profit is the main reason for being in business. As you will see on the next page, I have a very different view. I believe we need to be far more aware of what our world needs now and as a consequence of such awareness find our deep, heartfelt reason for doing what we do.

We also need to have far greater awareness of what is really going on in the hearts and minds of our stakeholders. Most leaders I meet do not really know what their employees and customers and other stakeholders feel and think. I know of no better way than *management by wandering around* to find out.
This is Sparkenation 30.

The other great awareness we must have is to really know for sure how compelling our story really is. This is Sparkenation 31.

Sparkenation 29.
What is the purpose of business, really?

Remember I use the words business and organisation interchangeably and I believe all organisations should be run like a business.

Normal

Ask most business people what is the purpose of their business and they will tell you *"to make a profit."*

Changing What's Normal

Ask me and I will give you a different answer.

I don't believe profit is a reason for being in business. I believe that profit is a result of being good at business! I am not saying we shouldn't make a profit, we should. However, how we make it and what we do with it, is becoming increasingly important to our stakeholders and to the value of our brand.

What is modern business really all about?

For me all businesses exist to define and deliver the value to all stakeholders that they demand, desire, and feel they deserve.

"...the future face of capitalism" say authors John Gerzema and Michael D'Antonio in their book *Spend Shift, "will be defined by delivering value and values."*

I have been saying this, and helping my clients to actually do this, for two decades, so it is nothing new. What could be new, however, is that the masses embrace this new kind of capitalism.

Where does one begin?

The massive fallout from the global financial crisis and the rise of people power in Egypt, Libya, and other places, means that many people are not only examining their values, they are also refusing to do business with people who they perceive are not in alignment with their values.
So the first step for me is to define our values.

We have all seen values displayed on walls and written in annual reports. The failure to live what is said and written is one of the biggest reasons for poor levels of employee and customer engagement. So defining our values is not just about words, it is about defining the actual behaviours.

In my experience, when agreed behaviours are measured as part of performance leadership and management, not only does greater accountability occur, the corresponding increases in engagement, and therefore productivity, mean profound changes in the delivery of value to stakeholders.

How do we define value to all stakeholders?

Broadly speaking there are two kinds of businesses. Firstly there are those who look for customers for their products and services. Secondly there are those providing products and services for their customers. I see a surge in the latter. Whatever kind of business we have, however, the simple rule is to ask stakeholders what they demand, desire, and feel they deserve.

Thinking of these three in terms of 'must haves', 'should haves', and 'nice to haves' is a useful way to begin.

"You will get all you want in life if you help enough other people get what they want", says Zig Ziglar

Creating shared value

Over the past 20 years I have made myself an authority in the concept of creating shared value or CSV, a business growth strategy referred to in a recent Harvard Business Review article by Michael E. Porter and Mark R. Kramer as *The Big Idea.*

I believe creating shared value begins with discovering shared view **in seven critical areas.**

1. Where we're going.
2. Why we're going there.
3. How we will get where we're going.
4. Who will do what and when and how.
5. The behaviours we will live in all our transactions and interactions.
6. Who we serve.
7. What those we serve demand, desire, and feel they deserve.

A great framework to ensure that we reach a shared view in these seven areas is the maxim for journalists and other investigators - the Five Ws and one H:

*   Who?   Who was involved?
*   What?   What happened (what's the story)?
*   Where? Where did it take place?
*   When?   When did it take place?
*   Why?   Why did it happen?
*   How?   How did it happen?

I love the words of Rudyard Kipling in his *Just So Stories for Little Children* (1902), in which a poem accompanying the tale of *The Elephant's Child* begins with:

> *I keep six honest serving-men*
> *(They taught me all I knew);*
> *Their names are What and Why and When*
> *And How and Where and Who.*

For simple understanding of organisational life and how to change it, I add 'Now' to these famous six and also prefer the order to be: Now, Where, Why, How, Who, What, and When.

We will explore my remaining sparkenations into organisational change in this order.

Possibility Action:

To get ready for your exploration of where you are now in your business I recommend you take time out to watch and reflect on my story: *Are your values on your wall lived in the hall?* You can access it at www.changingwhatsnormal.com/vault/

Do your work.

Now

Sparkenation 30.
Management by Wandering Around

Normal

Many leaders and managers are out of touch with what's really going on inside their organisations.   And many employees are afraid to tell them.

Changing What's Normal

My experience that day that you have just watched and reflected on in my video *Are your values on your wall lived in the hall?* occurred some 15 years ago and caused me to return to a modis operandi I had learned as a young manager some 20 years earlier. It was popularised by Tom Peters and called *Management by Wandering Around.*

This concept of *management by wandering around* was created by Hewlett Packard and it meant staying in direct touch with the folk who do the work.

I didn't know it in the seventies, however I was blessed in the those early days of my corporate career, that my mentors practiced *management by wandering around* and I followed in their footsteps. Doing so was a major factor in my success as a branch manager and later as a regional manager and corporate executive.

When I look back, I am amazed that I didn't follow this practice in my early years as a adviser/consultant.   Then again, as Alan Weiss says *"I am am amazed at how stupid I was two weeks ago!"*

That day in the foyer of my client's offices stopped me in my tracks and I immediately returned to *management by wandering around*!

Possibility Actions:

In the online learning vault please check out the link to Tom Peter's insights into *management by wandering around.*

There is also a link to 12 great guidelines for *management by wandering around* by the the folk at Futurecents.

You can access these links at www.changingwhatsnormal.com/vault/

> *"I learned that unless you get to know people*
> *and stand beside them as they work, you will find out only*
> *what they believe you want to know."*
> Kevin Roberts, Worldwide CEO of Ideas Company
> Saatchi & Saatchi

If you do not hold a leadership or management position please reflect on the following:

- ✓ Authentic leadership and management are not about position.
- ✓ Leadership and management are everyone's business. We are all leading and managing all day, every day, in every aspect of our lives.

I define Leadership as:
the art of inspiring people to bring everything remarkable that we are, that special, unique human being that each of us is (1 of 106 billion!), to everything we do.

Leadership falters without management.

I define Management as: the practice of making it simple for people to bring everything remarkable that we are to everything we do.

If you are person who has a leadership/management position what could you immediately change in order to embrace more of the art of leadership and the practice of management?

If you do not have an official position, you are still leading and managing. What could you immediately change in order to embrace more of the art of leadership and the practice of management?

Do your work.

Sparkenation 31.
Is your story a sparkenation?

Normal

Stories about organisations in the media and many communiques put out by organisations themselves are actually spin rather than authentic stories.

Changing What's Normal

I practice *management by wandering around* before every assignment.

Before presenting a tailored talk, providing mentoring, or leading a change program, I assess the compelling nature, or otherwise, of the story of the organisation and the individuals I will work with.

The answers I discover tell me much about where the organisation is now as well as where it is possible for the organisation to go.

I research what I refer to as the 7 R's of reality:
Remarkability, Reputation, Relevance, Reason, Remedies, Reliability, and Referability.

In my research I am seeking authentic answers to the questions that follow:

Remarkability

What is it that the people do that is remarkable i.e. conspicuously extraordinary?

In two extraordinary books *Purple Cow* and one I have already referred to, *Linchpin*, Seth Godin makes a strong case for differentiation in the modern world by being remarkable.

I love both the *purple cow* and *linchpin* ideas. As I meet people, talk to their internal and external customers and other stakeholders, I am looking for actions that stand out like a purple cow would in a field and, I am searching for ways of being that mean people would be very hard to replace.

How remarkable would I find you to be?

Reputation

How authentic and without spin is the organisation's reputation?

When I read vision, mission, and values statements and the like on walls and in publications such as annual reports I want to know, and I find out, how well the words are lived in real, everyday transactions and interactions.

How well would I find you living your words?

Relevance

How well does the organisation deliver value to all its stakeholders?

For me all organisations exist to deliver the value to their stakeholders that they demand, desire, and feel that they deserve.

How well are you delivering value to all your stakeholders?

Reason

What is the organisation's real reason for being in business?

As I have stated most people's answer - *"for profit"*.

And again I say, for me, profit is not a reason for being in business, rather, profit is a result of being good at business.

There is nothing wrong or evil about making a profit. However, if it is your sole reason for being in business I think you are in trouble. If your main game is profit I suggest your business will follow the same fate as the dinosaurs.

What I really want to know is what is the organisation's cause?

In his rap on an excellent book *The Culting of Brands* by Douglas Atkin, Geoff McDonald asks *"What do you want to have happen? If you're not out to cause anything then you might as well go back to bed."*

My cause is to co-create a world where every human being has their basic human needs met.

In 2007 I was privileged to speak to members of the board of Oxfam Trading Australia. While waiting in their boardroom I copied down the words of a poster on the wall by Community Aid Abroad. It was headed *'Basic human rights for all'* and was created long before the concept of corporate social responsibility had gained any momentum. It read:

> *enough to eat*
> *clean water*
> *a livelihood*

a home
an education
health care
a safe environment
protection from violence
equality of opportunity
a say in the future

Tears welled in my eyes as I read these words, for they capture what I stand for and explain why I got up this morning and why I rise with passion in my eyes every morning and go out into the world to inspire and influence people in whatever you do to be doing it for the good of people and our planet.

Indeed this is why I wrote this book.

That day, in the Oxfam Trading Boardroom, a seed was planted in my heart and mind that grew to become the *differencemakers community*.

What's your cause?

We will explore reason and cause more in the section on Why.

Remedies

Do the organisation's products/services provide solutions for customers and society's challenges and problems?

The former Vice-President and Chief Designer at Nokia, Frank Nuovo says *"Design in its simplest form is the activity of creating solutions."*

How many solutions have you designed?
How many problems are you preventing?

Reliability

How reliable is the organisation's service charter?

Wherever possible, when I am researching organisations before working with them, I physically walk the full supplier-customer chain.   I want to know how reliable is every aspect.   What promises are people making all the way along the chain and how well are the promises being delivered on?

How reliable would I find all aspects of your service delivery?

Referability

Do customers/clients rave about their experience of the organisation?

I find out what people are saying about the company and how many different places they are saying it, including social media outlets such as Facebook, LinkedIn, and Twitter, and outlets specific to the industry.

I am also very interested in how the organisation is helping their stakeholders to say good things in genuine ways.

The answers I discover tell me how referable the organisation is.

How referable are you?

Get your Remarkability, Reputation, Relevance, Reason, Remedies, Reliability, and Referability right for you and your story will be a sparkenation to others.

Possibility actions:

Answer honestly the following questions.

What is it that your people do that is remarkable i.e. conspicuously extraordinary?

How authentic and without spin is your organisation's reputation?

How well does your organisation deliver value to all its stakeholders?

What is your organisation's deep reason for being in business?

How many solutions to your customers' problems have you designed?

How many of society's problems are you preventing?

How referable are you?

Your authentic answers to these questions will help you get an accurate view of where you are Now.

To be really certain of the authenticity of your answers you might engage me, or someone like me, to provide you with non biased viewpoints.

If you do not hold a formal leadership or management position, you are still a leader and a manager, right? You are indispensable, right? What could you do to ensure your organisation's answers to the questions above are authentic? Speak up.

Do your work.

Be clear. Sparkenations 32 - 37.

We are much in the grip of short-termism particularly in business and politics where the focus is on the next quarterly result or the next election.

The greatest change I have seen in my lifetime, to the detriment of humanity, is that society has become part of the economy instead of the other way around.

To combat climate change, to prepare for the sustainable future of our children and our grandchildren, and to ensure the basic human rights of every human being are met, we need to change what's normal and to dramatically rethink where we are going.

Every successful business needs:

    ✓ A 'Plan A' for a sustainable future.

    ✓ Four key answers that will determine our future and the future of every human being who follows in our footsteps.

    ✓ An operating model that is as much about solving society's problems as it is about anything else.

    ✓ Ways to take and manage calculated risks.

    ✓ To end a preoccupation with self-interest and embrace enlightened self-interest.

    ✓ Principle based leadership and management.

These are the subjects of Sparkenations 32 - 37.

Where

Sparkenation 32.
Do you have a Plan A for where you're going?

Normal

Many organisations I have researched confuse slogans with their story.

Australia's big 4 banks had interesting slogans.

The Commonwealth Bank's slogan was *"Determined to be different"* and every day for months it seemed their slogan featured in numerous TV advertisements.

I find the slogan odd. I don't want to do business with people who are determined to be different; I want to do business with people who are different. And my personal experience of this bank is that they are not different, rather they are the same as every other bank!

Is your slogan authenticated by your story, or is it aspirational rather than actual?

When stories don't match slogans, brand value suffers. It is all very well to be aspirational, as *"determined to be different"* is. However, being aspirational when it comes to our slogans, tag lines, or value propositions is for me a dangerous practice. Of course, when our one-line positioning statement is actual and present tense, and we don't deliver, we are in even more trouble!

Think very carefully about what you say about yourself and your organisation. Only say what you will deliver.

The ANZ Bank had the slogan *"We live in your world"*. I have no idea what this means so they are unlikely to attract me as a customer.

Westpac Bank said *"We're a bank you can bank on"*. I have no idea what this means either. I bank with them more because they bought out the banks I've banked with for many years, than because I'm attracted by anything they say.

Do the people who you want to be your customers/clients get your slogan?

The National Australia Bank had the slogan *"more give, less take"*. I find this also an odd slogan for a bank when most people think of banks as more take, less give! Of course if National Australia Bank is delivering, then they would be standing out from the crowd. I can't comment as I am not one of their customers.

The NAB seems to also be embracing another slogan, *"we've broken up with other banks"*. This could be a real differentiator. Time will tell if it is just a slogan or a compelling story.

The bottom line is this:
Is your slogan authenticated by your story, i.e. by what you actually do?

Changing What's Normal

The British retailer Marks and Spencer also have a slogan:
"Doing the right thing".
From what I can tell their slogan is matched by their story.

Marks and Spencer launched what they call *"Plan A"* in January 2007, setting out 100 commitments to achieve within 5 years.
They boldly say *"there is no Plan B!"*
Marks and Spencer have recently extended their Plan A to 180 commitments with the goal to achieve these by 2015. They have the ultimate goal of becoming the world's most sustainable major retailer.

Possibility Action:

Please go to the links in the online learning vault and download Marks and Spencer's *Plan A* and begin to create your own.

You can access these links at www.changingwhatsnormal.com/vault/

If you are an employee, answer this question. What could you do to help your organisation create a *Plan A* for a sustainable future?

Do your work.

Sparkenation 33.
Four key questions to answer
that may well determine your future

Normal

Most businesses are conventional and attached to doing things as they always have. Very few organisations are truly innovative.

Changing What's Normal

Fast Company's 50 most innovative companies list for 2011 is very insightful into the future of business.

Fast Company's introduction to their list says in part:
"...world will be ruled by the kinds of companies on this list. They're non-dogmatic, willing to scrap conventional ideas. ...They're willing to fail. They know what they stand for."

Possibility Actions:

Check out Fast Companies 50 most innovative companies via the online learning vault. www.changingwhatsnormal.com/vault/

Reflect on what these companies are doing and answer these questions:

How non-dogmatic are you?
How non-conventional are you?
How much are you willing to fail?
What do you stand for?

If you are an employee, what are your answers to these questions? And what could you do today to help your organisation stand out from the crowd?

Your answers to these questions and how you act on your answers may well determine your future.

Do your work.

Sparkenation 34.
Is the co-operative business model
one you could emulate?

Normal

Since a group headed by Gro Harland Brundtland defined sustainability for the United Nations in 1987, and John Elkington invented the triple bottom line (social responsibility, environmental sustainability, economic prosperity, or people, planet, and profit) in the 90's, many leaders have moved to operate more sustainable businesses. However, sustainability is still not the normal business model the world needs it to be.

Changing What's Normal

The Co-operative Group is the UK's largest mutual retailer and they are changing what's normal.

In the UK, at the time of writing, they are the fifth largest food retailer, the third largest retail pharmacy chain, the number one provider of funeral services, and the largest independent travel business.

The Co-operative Group also has strong market positions in banking and insurance. The Group employs 120,000 people, has 5.5 million members and around 4,800 retail outlets.

I read the following on The Co-operative Group's website:

The Co-operative model

Like any business, we want to be a commercial success. However, even more important to us is the way that we do business, and the way that we use our profits. We believe that we should offer our customers both value and values. Which makes us a bit different.

Our members are our owners; they tell us what is important to them and we listen and act on it. It's part of our model: as a consumer co-operative, we run our business for the benefit of our members.

That means our members are involved in democratic decision-making, and we re-invest in our business – share of the profits - sharing profits with our members. Our members also set a social and campaigning agenda that we support. In fact - because our members wanted it - we've become pioneers in areas such as fairtrade and combating climate change. Of course, the more commercially successful we are, the more we can do to give back to the communities we serve and to influence the wider world.

Possibility actions:

In the online learning vault www.changingwhatsnormal.com/vault/ there is a link to an article by Adam Jupp in the *Manchester Evening News*, 14th December 2010, in which Chief Executive Peter Marks is quoted as saying *"The Co-operative Group is aiming for 20 million members by 2020."*
Achieving this goal would mean this organisation would be serving one third of the UK's population!
There is also a link in the online learning vault to The Co-operative Group's website.

Whatever your role in your organisation, what principles of a co-operative could you emulate? Decide and do your work.

Sparkenation 35.
What are you prepared to risk
to fulfill the dreams you have
for your organisation?

Normal

Most business leaders fail to consider all the 'what if' scenarios of their actions and, therefore when crisis comes, they are slow to act and usually fail miserably to meet the challenge and everyone suffers, often except them.

Changing What's Normal

I read this incredible story in a *Strategy + Business* article, a publication by Booz & Co on 4th February 2011.

> *One night in 1973, Fred Smith, the founder of the FedEx Corporation, decided to gamble, literally, on the future of his company. Short of funds to pay for airline fuel, Smith hopped a weekend flight to Las Vegas and took the company's last US$5,000 to the blackjack table. By Monday morning, he had the $24,000 he needed, and then some. Nearly four decades later, FedEx is a regular on Fortune magazine's 100 Best Companies to Work For list. According to the authors of this paper, there may be a connection between the company's dramatic story of survival and its high level of employee commitment.*

The article goes on to detail the results of a series of four experiments, where researchers explored how reflecting counter factually on an institution's origins - that is, considering 'what if' scenarios - can influence stakeholders' actions and commitment.

I found it all fascinating.

Possibility Actions:

Read the full *Strategy + Business* article. There is a link to it in the vault at www.changingwhatsnormal.com/vault/

Then answer these questions:

What are you prepared to risk to fulfill the dreams you have for yourself and/or your organisation? I am not suggesting, for one minute, that you take the company funds and go to a casino! I am asking you, what gambles will you take?

How many 'what if' scenarios have you considered about where you, or your organisation, are going that would enable you to effectively manage the risks you take?

How fast do you or your organisation turn disaster or adversity into something good for all your stakeholders?

Do your work.

Sparkenation 36.
Are you driven by
enlightened self-interest?

Normal

Most people and particularly leaders of organisations are driven by self-interest. Many leaders have out-of-control egos and somehow get rewarded for their blunders due to short-sighted performance contracts.

Changing What's Normal

I make a critical observation about organisations which I see as great, such as Marks and Spencer and The Co-operative Group; their leaders are driven by enlightened self-interest.

The following entries are found at Wikipedia.

Enlightened self-interest is a philosophy in ethics which states that persons who act to further the interests of others (or the interests of the group or groups to which they belong), ultimately serve their own self-interest.

It has often been simply expressed by the belief that an individual, group, or even a commercial entity will "do well by doing good".

In contrast to enlightened self-interest is simple greed or the concept of "unenlightened self-interest", in which it is argued that when most or all persons act according to their own myopic selfishness that the group suffers loss as a result of conflict, decreased efficiency because of lack of cooperation, and the increased expense each individual pays for the protection of their own interests.

All over the world I see 'unenlightened self-interest' destroying businesses, families, lives in general, and of course, being in the grip of 'unenlightened self-interest' means we are not yet able to avoid the catastrophes caused by our inability and unwillingness to live in harmony with our planet.

The good news is that I have also seen productivity and positivity go through the roof, and the changing of what's normal for the good of people and our planet, when the awesome power of 'enlightened self-interest' is at work.

Is 'enlightened self-interest' driving you? Could you do more for your world and therefore for yourself?

How many of your actions yesterday feathered your own nest and cost somebody else something they didn't want to give away?

A win for me, for you, for others, and the world in general is possible, it all depends on what intention is driving us.

Possibility Actions:

A powerful way to examine our motives is to reflect on the harmony you have between WIIFM (What's in it for me?) and WIMFY (What's in me for you?). **How in harmony are you?**

The Harvard Business Review blog of 12th March 2010 makes very interesting reading and reports that Indian companies are doing well because they do good.

What I find particularly interesting about this *HBR blog* by Peter Cappelli is the findings:

> *My colleagues and I recently completed a study of Indian businesses based around interviews with the leaders of 100 of the biggest companies in India (the basis of our book The India Way.)*

> *Every executive interviewed described the main objective of their company in terms of a social mission.*

"Business cannot survive in societies that fail." says Bjorn Stigson, President, World Business Council for Sustainable Development.

As you get clear on where you are going to take your organisation please carefully consider what is driving you and how what you make, provide, and do, is impacting on your world.

If you are an employee please carefully consider who it is you are working for and have the courage to leave if your organisation is not driven by enlightened self-interest.

If you decide to stay what will you do to make a difference in your organisation?

There are 142 possible actions for you to consider taking to operate a business that is good for people, our planet, and for profit in my ebook *Differencemakers - how doing good is great for business.* There is a link to download this ebook in the vault www.changingwhatsnormal.com/vault/

Do your work.

Sparkenation 37.
Authenticity and accuracy

Normal

Most leaders' view of where their organisation is at right now is a far cry from reality.

Changing What's Normal

The gap between Now and Where causes either creative tension, so described by Peter Senge in his excellent work *The Fifth Discipline*, or negative stress. You might now be feeling one or the other, or perhaps a bit of both!

Creative tension is more likely when we have a realistic view of where we are now and a clear and realistic vision of where we are going.

In almost all of the organisations I have worked with there has been, at the beginning, an unrealistic view of Now and an unclear vision of Where.

It is also human nature to put a positive spin on things, particularly when it comes to articulating the current performance of our organisations.

How often have you heard a CEO, when briefing financial analysts, not put a positive spin on the current state of their company even when everyone knows it's bad? My answer would be "not very often".

Of course one of the reasons that the whole financial system of the world almost collapsed during the recent Global Financial Crisis was the fact that the true state of affairs of many banks and other financial institutions was either not known or not truthfully communicated!

7 characteristics of the best companies

One of the great books written about the successful present and future of business, in my view, is *Firms of Endearment.* Authors Raj Sisodia, David B Wolfe, and Jag Sheth, put forward 7 characteristics in the book that differentiate the best companies from the rest as follows:

> *freely challenge industry dogma*
> *create value by aligning stakeholder interests*
> *are willing to break traditional tradeoffs*
> *operate with a long-term perspective*
> *favor organic growth to growing by mergers and acquisitions*
> *blend work with play*
> *reject traditional marketing models*

Possibility Actions:

Rate your organisation against the above 7.

Truthful answers to each of the above seven characteristics will give you an indication as to how accurate your view is of where you are now and will help you to make decisions about where you want to go.

Also rate your organisation against what have become known as the *Page Principles* on the next page.

1. *tell the truth*
2. *prove it with action*
3. *listen to the customer*
4. *manage for tomorrow*
5. *conduct public relations as if the whole company depends on it*
6. *a company's true character is expressed by its people*
7. *remain calm, patient and good-humored.*

Do your work.

Be inspiring. Sparkenations 38 - 41.

Most organisational mission statements are boring and uninspiring because they fail to capture the deep and abiding reason as to Why the organisation really exists.

When we understand our big Why and don't confuse what we do with why we do it, we are on the threshold of doing the profound. Sparkenations 38 and 39 expand on these concepts.

Sparkenations 40 and 41 are all about turning our Why into something that truly inspires our stakeholders and therefore engages them.

Why

Sparkenation 38.
Why must come before How

Normal

It is normal for most of the people I meet, who know where they are now and where they want to be, to jump straight to deciding how they are going to get there.

Changing What's Normal

Changing what's normal needs a Why before How because when we really get our Why we may change our Where!

The work you have done so far will have helped you. It's time now to get really clear about the deep reason or reasons your organisation exists.

Missions matter - mission statements don't

I came across a brilliant blog via a discussion on LinkedIn group *Association & Convention Innovators*. The blog by Dan Pallotta in Harvard Business Review *Do You Have a Mission Statement, or Are you on a Mission?* hits the target on why some organisations are thriving, others are barely surviving, and some are going south at a rapid rate - talk and no action.

I shared my thoughts with you on the pointlessness of vision, mission, and value statements unless they are lived when you watched the video of my experience, *Are your values on your wall lived in the hall you* (Sparkenation 29).

In a groundbreaking book *Start With Why,* Simon Sinek says:
"People don't buy WHAT we do, they buy WHY we do it."

What's your Why, your mission, your cause?
And, did you leap out of bed today with it at the forefront of
your mind? And, are you living it, every minute, of every day?

Possibility Actions:

In the online learning vault www.changingwhatsnormal.com/
vault/ there is a link to Dan Pallotta's blog referred to on the
previous page. I highly recommend you study it and use it to help
you to clarify your Why.

There is also a link in the vault to Simon Sinek's *Start With Why*
TED talk. If watching this and reflecting doesn't help you to be
really clear on your Why then go further and buy the book or call
me and I will help you.

Please go no further until you are crystal clear on Why your
organisation exists.

This is really, really important because one of the truly great
lessons of philosophy is:

> *"He who has a why to live can bear almost any how."*
> Friedrich Nietzsche

> which has been popularised to mean

> *"When we understand the WHY*
> *the HOW is easy!"*

If you are an employee. please take these actions as well.

Doing so will really help you to decide if the organisation employing you is really the place you can belong to.   If it is, terrific! If not, time to find a place where you can really belong.

Do your work.

Sparkenation 39.
When profit is a reason,
we confuse what we do
with why we do it

Skip this insight if you are absolutely certain about your Why.

Normal

I well remember the moment, 20 years ago, when I said publicly for the first time, *"profit is not a reason for being in business, profit is a result of being good at business."*

I was speaking to a group of Chief Executives and although no-one laughed out loud there were plenty of smirks and internal chuckles. There still are, however not as many!

Changing What's Normal

20 years ago I was stating a notion I had. Today it is a firm conviction that I have seen to be true hundreds of times over.

Now let me be crystal clear. I am not saying profit is bad, or that we shouldn't make a profit. Profit is good and if you aren't making one in your business then something is seriously wrong with how you are doing business.

What I am saying is that profit is a result of being good at business not a reason for being in business. To be confused about this means we get very fuzzy about How and the consequence is that we fail to perform at optimum levels.

Paradoxically, when we fail to perform at optimum levels, profits are less than they should be and therefore we are unable to reinvest appropriately in our business nor do what we really could for society.

If you are not achieving the results you want in your business right now, more than likely you are not really clear about Why you are in business.

Possibility Actions:

Here are some questions to answer that will help you get clear, if you are not already, on why you are in business:

What gets you out of bed in the morning?
What difference are you making to the communities in which your business operates?
What drives you?
What kind of legacy will you leave?
What is the purpose of your life?
What do you really care about?
How could you thrive in your business and solve a problem in your world at the same time?

I am in business to change what's normal because I believe the status quo no longer serves humanity well.

Why are you in business?

Making the shift from what to Why

Seeing our organisations in terms of our social and/or environmental mission and embracing enlightened self-interest requires many of us to shift our focus from:

results to reasons
profit to purpose
profit to people, planet, and profit
outcomes to processes
brand to lovemark (thank you Kevin Roberts of
Saatchi & Saatchi)
shareholders to stakeholders
me to we
success to significance
values to virtues (unless values are verbs they are just
meaningless words)
selling proposition to value proposition
competition to collaboration

My clear observation of the past 20 years is that strong reasons precede strong results.

Being crystal clear on Why we do what we do is the first step to moving from where we are Now to Where we're going with certainty.

Do your work.

How

Sparkenation 40.
Create a manifesto

Normal

Most mission statements lack meaning or they read like they could apply to any organisation.

Changing What's Normal

The fortnight beginning April 11th 2011 was an amazing period of synchronicity for me. I was thinking about this sparkenation.

Out of the blue, a colleague from Ireland, Liviu Caliman, sent me a link about the work of Futerra, a leader in research and communications about sustainability. There are a lot of brilliant resources at Futerra.

Then I saw a tweet by another colleague, Geoff McDonald (The Book Rapper) from Australia about his manifesto project. The aim of this project is to create a freely available resource of 1000 manifestos. Why? To inspire people to stand up, make change happen and create a world that works.

I posted my 'changing what's normal' manifesto on Geoff's site on April 14th.

On April 18th yet another colleague, Maree Harris, posted a blog titled *Dr. Shine: Making a Difference Shining Shoes,* refreshing my memory about the wonderful work on manifestos by *changethis.com*

Possibility Actions:

Visit the online learning vault www.changingwhatsnormal.com/vault/ and check out the links to Futerra, the blog by Maree Harris, and read as many of the manifestos on *changethis.com* that strike you as synergetic. There is a link to *changethis.com* in the vault. At the very least download *Art of the Start* manifesto by Guy Kawasaki.

Guy says:

> *MAKE MEANING.*
> *The best reason to start an organization is to make meaning—to create a product or service that makes the world a better place. So your first task is to decide how you can make meaning.*

> *MAKE MANTRA.*
> *Forget mission statements; they're long, boring, and irrelevant. No one can ever remember them—much less implement them. Instead, take your meaning and make a mantra out of it. This will set your entire team on the right course.*

More on mantras in my next sparkenation.

I also highly recommend you subscribe to Geoff McDonald's manifesto email list and you will receive an excellent ebook about how to write your manifesto the contents of which cover:

1. *Manifestos are primal*
2. *Manifestos terminate the past*
3. *Manifestos create the future*
4. *Manifestos trigger communities*

5. *Manifestos define us*
6. *Manifestos antagonise others*
7. *Manifestos inspire being*
8. *Manifestos provoke action*
9. *Manifestos command presence*

There is a link to Geoff's ebook in the vault.

Do your work. Write your own personal manifesto and one for your organisation.

Sparkenation 41.
Breaking your manifesto down
to six words

Normal

Ask most employees of any organisation what the strategy is for the organisation's growth and well-being and you will get a blank look.

Changing What's Normal

Strategy for me is the How that we determine which, when executed, will take us from where we are to where we want to be.

Defining strategy and agreeing on what it means however, presents a challenge for most people. In fact, coming up with a strategy in the first place is just as challenging, if not more so.

In their book *Strategy Safari* (Prentice Hall 2002), authors Henry Mintzberg, Bruce Ahlstrand, and Joseph Lampel explore the great aspects of strategy including

> *the five Ps of plan, ploy, pattern, perspective, position, and ten separate schools of strategy, environmental (strategy as a reactive process), cognitive (strategy as mental process), entrepreneurial (strategy as a visionary process), power (strategy as a process of negotiation), positioning (strategy as an analytical process), cultural (strategy as a collective process), planning (strategy as a formal process), learning (strategy as an emergent process), design (strategy as a process of conception), and configuration (strategy as a process of transformation).*

Their book argues that strategy is not just one of these, rather it embraces all of these. And it may.

For me, however, to change what's normal across a broad base means simplifying strategy so that those who have to execute it (usually employees), get it, and own it, and are therefore more likely to execute it.

Six words may be all you need to describe your strategy

The harsh reality is that most great strategies fail to get executed. For me the key reasons for this are, firstly, strategy and the plan to achieve it are confused with one another, and secondly, the execution plan isn't clear to those responsible for the execution.

Strategic planning is an oxymoron. Your strategy and your plan to achieve it should be thought about separately.

I define strategy as: the reference points from which we make all the key decisions about exchanging value. Exchanging value is what a business is all about. You demand, desire, and feel you deserve something from me and you are prepared to give me something in exchange for it.

As a general rule six words are all we need as triggers for our reference points.

The great writer Ernest Hemingway
thought the following were six of his best words:

"For Sale: Baby shoes, Never worn."

Inspired by Hemingway, and the great work at Smith Magazine and their '6 word memoirs' project, my friend, colleague, and founder of Leaders Cafe 2020, Kwai Yu, asked the following question on a LinkedIn discussion: *"Who are you? Could you tell the story of you in six words?"*

Kwai received hundreds of extraordinary responses which inspired me to think about how I could best teach people about strategy in ways that would mean greater ownership and therefore greater likelihood of execution.

When I began experimenting with my concept of a 'six word strategy', my first six words for my business were:
Enlightened self-interest, differencemaking, self-sufficiency, rituals, harmony.

These words helped me to position myself as a go to person for people who want to do well by doing good, make a difference, be self-sufficient, realise sustainability is an outcome of a journey, and that living in harmony with each other and our planet is possible.

My strategy then evolved into something much more practical for me with my six words being: challenges/causes, channels, connections, conversations, core.

By understanding the **challenges** facing people in my target markets and the **causes** of these challenges and by sharing my research, insights, and results through digital **channels** such as blogs, slideshares, podcasts, and videos, I made a lot of **connections** with people I wouldn't have otherwise connected with. They connected with me on LinkedIn or signed up at various entry points to beginning relationships, such as my monthly ezine, completing one of my online pulse checks.

Following this strategy meant I could have **conversations** in the real world with many more people than I was having previously and a percentage of these conversations, of course, led to **core business**.

Now I don't expect you to fully understand my strategy which has since evolved further to my current six words: rolls-royce relationships lead to rolls-royce buyers. These six words have become my mantra. These words will probably mean very little to you. **My point is that if we do the work we can come up with a simple yet profound strategy for moving from where we are to Where we want to be. One that fully embraces our Why.**

"We don't have a strategic plan ... instead we simply decide what makes sense for our owners."
Warren Buffet 1995 report to shareholders

Possibility actions:

Deciding strategic positioning is the starting place for determining strategy in my view.

One guru of strategy, Michael E. Porter, would say strategy is about positioning. He says:

> *"Strategy is the creation of a unique and valuable position involving a different set of activities.*
>
> *Competitive strategy is about being different. It means deliberately choosing a different set of activities to deliver a unique mix of value."*

There are really only two ways to gain a strategic position in a market; do what your competitors don't do, or do what your competitors do, yet, do it differently, better, or more uniquely. Where are you positioned in your market? How can you improve your strategic positioning?

Take time to answer these questions and in particular ask your employees, in a variety of ways, what they feel and think.

A strategy created without the people who will execute it is doomed to fail.

After you have completed your research, put a team together to come up with your six words and then road test them with your employees to ensure that what you have come up with is what they will buy into, own, and act on. You might even run some kind of fun event where everyone is involved in creating your six words.

If you are an employee, get on the team!

As a part of many conference and in-house presentations for clients, I often include a short exercise where people create strategies. I have been delighted, moved, and inspired by the profound 'six word strategies' that people create.

For further inspiration on your six words check out the link in the vault www.changingwhatsnormal.com/vault/ to Smith Magazine and their amazing '6 word memoirs' project.
Do your work.

"If you can't write your movie idea on the back of a business card,
you ain't got a movie."
Samuel Goldwyn

Be attractive. Sparkenations 42 - 45

A large number of organisations fail to be attractive to their stakeholders because they do not know exactly what people demand, desire, and feel that they deserve. Sparkenation 42 takes a look at this so that you can be sure you are beyond assumption.

Once we are certain we know what our stakeholders want, we need to ensure that we remain attractive by having a supplier-customer chain that delivers to people what they want. This is explored in Sparkenation 43.

Integral to delivery is recruiting the people who are passionate for your cause and retaining such people. We explore this in detail in Sparkenation 44.

Finally in this section we take a look at how to be attractive by capturing strategy and execution plans on one page.

Who, What, and When

You are now clear on where you are Now, Where you're going, Why you're going there, and How (strategy) you will make the journey. Now comes the crucial bit, actually making it happen!

Sparkenation 42.
Assumption:
You know what your stakeholders want

Normal

Most organisations don't actually know what their stakeholders really want. Many have never asked them.

Changing What's Normal

Before we explore executing your strategy, it is vital that you know what your stakeholders demand, desire, and feel they deserve from you. The following are the common stakeholders for the typical organisation that I partner with:

Governments
NGOs (Non government organisations)
Communities
Shareholders/Owners
Board members
Leaders
Employees
Customers/Clients
Suppliers
External performance partners
Financiers
Our planet

When was the last time you surveyed your stakeholders? Are you certain you know exactly what they demand (must have), desire (should have), and feel they deserve (nice to have)?

If you cannot answer a resounding yes to these questions, you need to get about asking immediately, if not sooner.

Of particular interest to me, in my work with my clients, is knowing what employees really want and what customers/clients really want.

What Employees Really Want From Employers (my research)

- ✓ Appreciation. The eminent psychologist William James observed: *"The deepest craving of human nature is the need to be appreciated."*
- ✓ To be held to account via regular, constructive performance feedforward and feedback.
- ✓ Autonomy.
- ✓ Opportunity to master something.
- ✓ Role satisfaction.
- ✓ A feeling that their work contributes to a higher purpose.
- ✓ Knowing that their work is helping them to achieve their aspirations.
- ✓ Open, regular, truthful, information gathering and sharing.
- ✓ Remuneration perceived to be at least equal to effort.
- ✓ Trust and trustworthiness.
- ✓ Happy and healthy working environment.
- ✓ Fairness in all dealings.
- ✓ Flexibility.
- ✓ Hope for the future.

What Employees Really Want From Each Other (my research)

- ✓ Goal and strategy alignment.
- ✓ Promises kept.
- ✓ Open communication.
- ✓ Understanding of personal needs.
- ✓ Trust, trustworthiness, and confidence.
- ✓ Appreciation, support and encouragement.
- ✓ Authenticity.
- ✓ Sense of family.
- ✓ Acceptance of the merit of ideas.
- ✓ Mutual respect.

What customers/clients really want

Geoffrey James has sold and written hundreds of features, articles and columns for many publications including *Wired, Men's Health, Business 2.0, SellingPower, Brand World, Computer Gaming World, CIO, The New York Times.*

Geoffrey believes all customers want the same 12 things, regardless of who they are, who is selling to them or what they're buying. In my work over the past 20 years I would concur with every one of these.

1. *They want to feel important.*
2. *They want to be appreciated.*
3. *They want you to stop talking about yourself.*
4. *They want you to stop talking about your firm.*
5. *They want you to truly listen.*
6. *They want to be understood.*
7. *They want to teach YOU something.*
8. *They want and need your help.*

9. They want to buy something.
10. They want you to delight and surprise them.
11. They want to pretend they make logical decisions.
12. They want success and happiness.

These 12 were part of an article by Geoffrey James for *BNET.*
There is a link to the full article in the vault
www.changingwhatsnormal.com/vault/

Possibility Actions:

Continually make it your practice to informally and formally ask
all your stakeholders what it is that they demand, desire, and feel
that they deserve from you and then deliver.

I would strongly suggest that you develop a system for staying in
touch with your stakeholders because frequency and a sequence
are very important. You can read an overview of my system in the
vault www.changingwhatsnormal.com/vault/

Read Daniel Pink's excellent book *Drive – the surprising truth
about what motivate us.*

If you are an employee, continually ask and understand what the
people you serve want from you and help them to understand and
appreciate what you want from them.

Do your work.

Sparkenation 43.
Creating a supplier-customer chain structure

Normal

One of the biggest reasons for failure to execute strategy, that I have witnessed, is a poor structure and people not matched to roles. Equally any misunderstanding about who is serving who can have catastrophic consequences.

Changing What's Normal

"Who is serving who?" is the fundamental question that must be answered and from there ensuring 'the right people are in the right seat on the bus', a great metaphor from the book *Good to Great* by Jim Collins.

One of the great Japanese management thinkers and innovators Kaoru Ishikawa said: *"The customer is whoever gets your work next."* I find this to be a profound insight.

The Board of Directors of an organisation are serving the owners of the organisation and its leaders, who in turn are serving employees, who in turn are serving customers/clients. In the process all are also serving other stakeholders. The challenge we are all faced with is creating shared value for all stakeholders so that everyone wins.

Possibility Actions:

Create a map that details what all your stakeholders demand, desire, and feel that they deserve from you.

Next determine the roles that you would need people to fulfill to meet what your stakeholders want. Do not think about people you know while doing this, just think about what the roles are. Next create a role clarity statement for each role. There is a template in the vault www.changingwhatsnormal.com/vault/

Finally match people to roles.

Align systems with your structure

Much pain and a corresponding drop in productivity is caused by standard operating policies, procedures, and practices (SOPs) not accurately reflecting how things are in the real world.

Often SOPs have been written by consultants to help an organisation get the 5 ticks or whatever for an ISO standard and employees simply shake their heads in dismay, for there is no way that what is written can actually be achieved in an efficient and effective manner.

The best operations manuals I have seen have been written by the best employees. Who has written/writes yours? Do they accurately describe what happens?

If not. Do your work.

Carefully consider the unwritten ground rules or UGRs®
of your organisation.

UGRs® are the actual virtues of your organisation. Find out more about UGRs® and their creator Steve Simpson by clicking on the link in the vault www.changingwhatsnormal.com/vault/

Sparkenation 44.
Stop recruiting and retaining
the wrong people

Normal

In the great book previously referred to, *The Way We're Working Isn't Working*, authors Tony Schwartz, Jean Gomes and Catherine McCarthy, Ph.D., share results of a 2007 - 2008 global workforce study by Towers Perrin (now Towers Watson) involving some 90,000 employees from 18 countries as follows:

> *Only 20 percent of them felt fully engaged ...*
> *Forty percent were "enrolled," meaning capable but not fully committed, and 38 percent were disenchanted or disengaged.*

These statistics don't surprise me

I have asked approximately 1,000 CEO's over the past decade how many of their employees do they think are fully engaged in their organisation. I have asked them to use my definition of engagement i.e. people "bringing everything they are to everything they do on a consistent basis." The average answer has been 25% engaged, 65% open to persuasion, and 10% disengaged.

Some of Aon Hewitt's conclusions from its 2010 Employee Engagement 2.0 Study were:

✓ *Over 50% (of employees) are passive or actively disengaged.*
✓ *42% are not energized by their work.*
✓ *Only 43% trust in senior leadership.*
✓ *40% are generally stressed to the point of feeling burned out.*

Other conclusions that stood out for me were:

- ✓ *Only 33% rate their leadership as very or extremely effective in retaining the talent they need for the future.*
- ✓ *Less than one-third feel that leaders are very effective in hiring more productive employees.*

In Blessing White's *Employee Engagement Report 2011*, which reflects interviews with HR and line leaders as well as online survey responses of nearly 11,000 individuals from North America, India, Europe, Southeast Asia, Australia/New Zealand, and China, I note the following conclusions:

- ✓ *Fewer than 1 in 3 employees are Engaged. Of the 10,914 workers surveyed worldwide only 31% are Engaged.*
- ✓ *The Engaged stay for what they give; the Disengaged stay for what they get.*

What's going on?

My answer is that the following are norms:

- ✓ The majority of employees in the majority of organisations are not performing at their best which means that very few organisations are achieving what they are capable of.
- ✓ Many leaders have not tapped into why they are in business.
- ✓ Most people feel undervalued and under appreciated in their workplaces.
- ✓ A majority of strategies won't get executed because employees haven't bought into and don't own the strategy.
- ✓ Very few leaders are authentic and inspiring which is why only a minority are following them.

Changing What's Normal

Changing what's normal in organisational life means being really inspiring about where you are Now, Where you're going, Why you're going there, so that buy-in and ownership of your strategy by a majority of your employees, (the primary executors of your strategy) is simple.

Buy-in and ownership is all about employee engagement and such engagement begins with **only recruiting and retaining people who live your values and embrace your mission.**

Possibility actions:

Share your manifesto and your strategy with every prospective employee.
If you don't sense a fire in the belly and see passion in their eyes, do not employ them.

Explore the role clarity statement for the role you are recruiting for with the prospective employee.
If you don't sense a fire in the belly and see passion in their eyes, do not employ them.

If you are an engaged employee ask yourself what you can do to inspire others to become engaged. See more on this in Sparkenations 46 - 49.

If you are a disengaged employee ask yourself what can you do to become engaged. If you can't see a way forward, is it time for you to move on and find a place where you can belong?

Above all else, engagement is about what we give not what we get. The paradox is that the more we give without attachment to getting back, the more we get back!

Do your work.

In the sparkenations that follow we will explore key performance leadership and management tools for engaging new employees, re-engaging current employees who are not fully engaged, and letting go your disengaged employees who are unable or unwilling to step up to the mark.

Sparkenation 45.
Creating a snapshot of your strategy and your execution plan

Normal

What happens to strategic plans once they have been written? They generally go to the same place as lost socks and biros, never to be seen again until strategic planning season comes around again.

Changing What's Normal

Create documents people will refer to over and over.

Possibility Actions:

Take everything you have determined so far; where you are Now, Where you're going, Why you're going there, and How you will make the journey; and capture a snapshot of it all on one page. I have found this to be a very powerful exercise for myself personally and for many of my clients.

Visit the vault first www.changingwhatsnormal.com/vault/ and reflect on my one-page, and the one-page for one of my clients, 360 Private.

It is not important that you understand everything contained in these examples, what is important is the you get a feel for what you may need to include in your one-page. Do your work.

If you are an employee, collaborate with your bosses to create a document that makes sense to you and that you can refer to as integral to your work. Do your work.

Be engaged. Sparkenations 46 - 49

These sparkenations are about the keys to maximising employee engagement, namely:

✓ celebration and review (not appraisal) before planning.

✓ personal and business performance plans.

✓ making sure we do not confuse people with their performance.

✓ enhancing our gifts and the gifts of other people.

Sparkenation 46.
Cascading strategy down to
teams and individuals

Normal

Most strategic plans never leave the boardroom or the bottom left hand drawers of executive team members' desks.

Changing What's Normal

Assuming you have done the work appropriate for you to date, now is the time for the rubber to hit the road in terms of employee engagement.

I have met thousands of employees from a myriad of organisations, across many industries, and in many countries. Not once have I ever met an employee who was motivated by the organisation's goals as much as the owners or the leaders were.

Employees care about their own goals far more than yours. Something very powerful happens, however, when an employee feels that working with you is a key way to achieve their goals. The more people feel that you are helping them achieve what is vital and important to them, the more they will help you achieve what you feel is vital and important to you.

Personal and business performance plans are one way to achieve a shared view with your employees about their goals and yours and how both will be achieved.

Possibility Actions:

Meet with every one of your employees, or ensure your leaders do, and have a conversation with them that celebrates their achievements.

If you have never had such a conversation I highly recommend using the template in the vault www.changingwhatsnormal.com/vault/

Once you have completed this exercise, work with individuals and help them to create a personal and business performance plan for the next 90 days that, if executed, would mean people keep doing what they are currently doing well and make some improvements in areas where they currently could do better. Use the template in the vault if you wish. www.changingwhatsnormal.com/vault/

If you already have some kind of performance management system or process in place, then work out a way to incorporate the principles of what I am espousing here, namely:

Celebration comes **before** planning.
Performance plans that articulate **both** personal and business goals, and how they will be achieved, are imminently more powerful than either/or.

If you are an employee, instigate conversations with your boss about celebrating what you are doing well and could be doing better. Talk to your boss about creating a 90 day personal and business performance plan for yourself.

Do your work.

Sparkenation 47.
Appraisals are dead;
just not buried yet

Normal

Whilst working in the United Kingdom in February 2008, I was surprised at the amount of media concerning performance appraisals. One article in particular, in the *Sunday Times* of 24th February, grabbed my attention with the sub headline reading *"Managers need to be trained better in carrying out annual staff performance reviews ..."* The article went on to quote a recent survey by *Investors in People* which found that a third of employees think appraisals are a waste of time.

I have never been a fan of appraisals because I have rarely met an employee who enjoyed having one!

To leave a performance review for a year in the modern world is poor practice. Every 90 days is the norm for organisations which are changing what's normal and where the key is the informal feedback exchange that occurs daily. This means that the formal review is about celebrating performance and agreeing on the performance plan for the next 90 days. In the past year, I have found that, because of the speed of change, a formal performance review every 30 days is also common.

On the 8th of November 2010 I posed a question to my LinkedIn connections: *"How often are employees you know having formal performance reviews?"* More than 50% answered *"annually"*. Very few answered *"quarterly"* or better.

Changing What's Normal

One firm conclusion that I make after 20 years of helping my clients to develop and grow performance leadership and management systems that actually lead to performance improvement is that **human beings do not want to be appraised; they want to be appreciated**.

People also want to be held to account when their performance is less than it was planned that it would be.

To leave appreciation or being held to account for a year is an insult to humanity.

It is not training for managers in how to complete annual reviews that is needed. What is needed, and desperately in most quarters, is a complete rethink and redesign, and in some cases a complete relearning, about the essentials of effective performance leadership and management.

In my view, regardless of the system used, or the sophistication or otherwise of it, the essentials are:

- ✓ regular celebration of performance.
- ✓ personal and business performance plans that are aligned with the strategy and execution plan of the organisation.
- ✓ daily appreciation of people.
- ✓ holding people to account when appropriate or as the following technique illustrates helping people to hold themselves to account.

Possibility actions:

All of us have aspirations, and the greatest way I know to achieve them is to have a performance plan created with performance partners which is aligned with something greater than ourselves, and for other people to appreciate us when we do well and to help us hold ourselves to account when we perform less than we desire.

The great leaders who are changing what's normal, in my experience, are those who ask great questions. The poor leaders I witness are stuck in the status quo of giving answers.

I designed the 'Double A Technique' around asking great questions.

Effective use of the technique assumes employees buy into and own your strategy, particularly their piece of the execution plan, i.e. their personal and business performance plan.

The 'Double A Technique' can be downloaded in the vault, www.changingwhatsnormal.com/vault/ and is also detailed on the next page.

If you are an employee help your boss to ask great questions by asking them great questions yourself.

Do your work.

The Double A Technique

Ask: "How are things going?"

When you get a positive response:

Ask: "How does that make you feel?"
(be quiet and pay attention)

Then say, Great, Brilliant or whatever is appropriate.

Then ask: "Any other areas I can help you with?"
(be quiet and pay attention)

When you get a negative response

Ask: "What happened?" (be quiet and pay attention)

Then Ask: "What do you need to do to get back on track?"
(be quiet and pay attention)

Then Ask: "Is there anything I can do to help you?"
(be quiet and pay attention)

Finally, Ask: "Anything else?"
(be quiet and pay attention)

You can use this technique any time you meet informally with anyone with whom you have goal congruence and their permission to be their performance partner.

Sparkenation 48.
Confuse people with their performance
at your peril

Normal

The way most people work is counterproductive to doing great work. Some politicians trot out this line *"We don't negotiate with terrorists."*

Consider this: people are not terrorists.
Sure (tragically), some people commit terrorist acts.
And even good people do bad things occasionally!

Confuse people with their performance at your peril.
By calling people terrorists, politicians are setting up confrontation, and it's all down hill from there.

Changing What's Normal

Do you confuse people, the one-of-kind human being that each of us is, with what they do or don't do?

Recently I was helping a client deal with some poor performance issues, particularly with one individual. My client, in referring to this person, said *"He is such a dickhead most of the time."*

I am willing to bet that all of us have labeled someone like this.
I have.

I ran the following past my client:
"Despite all the ghastliness that is around, human beings are made for goodness."
Desmond Tutu

I then asked my client: *"Does Alan* (not his real name) *have all the skills to fulfill his role?"*

My client answered *"Yes I think so."*

I then asked: *"Is he willing to apply all his skills?"*

"Nope", was my clients answer.

Turns out, as is often the case with poor performance, 'Alan' was not clear on what was expected of him. His personal and business goals, and how he intended to achieve them, weren't even written down when I first spoke with him, therefore making it impossible to properly and professionally lead and manage for 'Alan', let alone him leading and managing for himself.

Does every employee at your place have their personal and business goals, and how they will achieve them, written down? Yes? Please proceed. No? Please go back to Sparkenation 46.

And is there alignment between each individual's personal and business goals, and how they will be achieved, with the strategy and the execution plan of your organisation?
Yes? Please proceed. No? Please go back to Sparkenation 45.

Possibility Actions:

Use the tools and templates offered in this book and the companion vault www.changingwhatsnormal.com/vault/

If you don't like them then please feel free to embrace the principles in your own way.

Move to performance periods that matter: i.e. 90 days, or even 30 days.

Move from appraising performance to having appreciation and accountability conversations with people.

If you are an employee, be brave and inspiring by taking the initiative and taking these actions yourself and you will inspire your bosses to appreciate you when you do well and hold you to account when your performance could be better.

Do your work.

Sparkenation 49.
Enhancing their gifts

Normal

I usually feel emotionally and physically ill when I meet leaders who are on a quest to change people into someone in their own image.

I once hated people trying to change me.   How about you? In fact I used to be so stubborn sometimes, knowing I should change something, that I wouldn't change because I perceived other people were driving the change, not me.

These days I ignore people trying to change me. I have concluded that what other people think of me is none of my business.

Trying to change other people is futile and is a slippery slope to self-destruction.   The good news is we can inspire others to change themselves by being change masters ourselves.

Changing What's Normal

A great way to lead i.e. inspire and influence, is to focus on enhancing people's gifts. This has much to do with coaching and mentoring.

I am often asked *"what is the difference between a coach and a mentor?"* My answer is that there doesn't need to be a difference in terms of labels, yet making a distinction can be very useful in terms of roles.

Coaching is concerned with competency: the skills needed to perform at optimum levels. **Good coaching is about maximizing skills.**

Mentoring is concerned with commitment: the will we need to perform at our best. **Good mentoring is about maximizing will.**

In the 90's I was President of the Tea Tree Gully District Cricket Club in Adelaide for six years and for four of those years Terry Jenner, who played cricket for Australia in the 70's, was the coach. It was the beginning of a life-long friendship with TJ as he was better known. Sadly, TJ passed way on 25th May 2011 after a long illness. He was my best friend and I miss him.

TJ believed his role as a coach was to *"Enhance the Gift"* of the people he coached. This is a beautiful phrase (from a storehouse of many from TJ) to describe both coaching and mentoring. We are drawing out what is already there.

TJ was widely acknowledged as the pre-eminent coach of his generation in his field of spin bowling. I was privileged, over two decades, to watch him work with many people with diverse gifts in both Australia and the United Kingdom, including his work with Shane Warne, regarded by most as the greatest bowler in the history of cricket. I have adopted many of TJ's philosophies and methodologies in my work as a mentor including:

"basics are beautiful"
"inch by inch is a cinch; yard by yard, too hard"
"if you practice the things that work, you get better at the things that work. If you practice the things that don't work, you get better at the things that don't work."

The Ancient Greek word for gift is charisma. When we coach and mentor well, people's charisma increases.

The higher the levels of charisma, or what I prefer to call personal significance, the greater the performance.

We all need coaches and mentors to help us inspire ourselves to be and do more. My whole life I have worked with and engaged mentors and make it my business to do so at least twice a year.

Recently a colleague introduced me as his mentor. I was flattered. Later on I asked him what mentor meant to him. He said, *"You help me maintain my attitude.   You are someone I can come to when I feel I need a lift or a sounding board."*

Are you a good coach and a good mentor?   Your people, including your children if you are a parent, need you to be.

I was a fan of Cathy Freeman, the indigenous Australian sprinter and 400 metre specialist, long before she won Olympic Gold. I was very interested to read her biographer Adrian McGregor talking about her *"mental delete button"*. Cathy used this to block out input that might disturb her focus.

Good coaches and good mentors help us to block out all the things that aren't of value to us in performing at our personal best.

Possibility Actions:

Take the Reality Check on the next page. Better still have those people who you coach and mentor assess your performance.

Good Coaching requires

✓ Ability to articulate how performance should be.

✓ Ability to share knowledge clearly and succinctly.

✓ Ability to create diverse, fun, practice methodologies.

✓ Ability to be tough yet fair.

✓ Ability to challenge people respectfully.

✓ Ability to separate problems from personality.

✓ Ability to be general with praise and specific with criticism.

Good Mentoring requires

✓ Willingness to influence others regarding the steps necessary to lift performance yet allow others to make their own decisions.

✓ Willingness to listen more than speak.

✓ Willingness to give advice but more to encourage people to find their own way.

✓ Willingness to experience delayed gratification.

✓ Willingness to give away hard earned wisdom.

If you are an employee, take the time and spend the energy identifying your gifts and incorporate enhancing them into your personal and business performance plan.

Be the kind of person, as an employee, who can be coached and mentored. Fulfill the roles of coaching and mentoring of your fellow employees where appropriate and in agreement with them.

Do your work.

Be authentic. Sparkenations 50 - 55

Very few people got out of bed this morning with an intention to make this a miserable or mediocre day!

When your day is not going according to plan I highly recommend that you check how authentic you are being in the areas listed below. These are the subject matter of Sparkenations 50 - 55:

- ✓ Are you making the decisions you have the ability and willingness to make?

- ✓ Are you empowered to make such decisions?

- ✓ Are you wooing and wowing people through the service you are providing them?

- ✓ In the various change initiatives that are happening in your organisation are you embracing the change/s authentically or are you resisting?

- ✓ Check to see that you are focused on giving rather than on getting.

- ✓ Ensure that you are taking control of the things you can control.

- ✓ Ask yourself are you acting to create shared value?

Sparkenation 50.
Decisions must be made where
and when it matters

Normal

Empowerment is a myth in most organisations and there is a lack of trust by most leaders in their people. Therefore decisions rarely get made where and when they matter the most.

Concerning major decisions, most organisations lack transparency in how decisions are made. Is it any wonder employee engagement levels are low?

> *"In my experience, when you go into most companies what you find is good people and bad management."*
> Kevin Roberts, Worldwide CEO of Ideas Company
> Saatchi & Saatchi

Key reasons why 50% of decisions fail
according to research by Dr Paul Nutt, Ohio State University:

> *Managers:*
> 1. *rush to judgment*
> 2. *misuse their resources*
> 3. *repeatedly use failure-prone tactics to make decisions*
> 4. *use power or persuasion and expect employees to follow - only successful one in every three decisions*

Changing What's Normal

On the next page is a decision-making model which I teach people

to get them started on effective decision-making.

I am staggered at the number of organisations who don't have a decision-making process and so I designed the following as a starting place. Usually, wise people evolve it into something that works well for them.

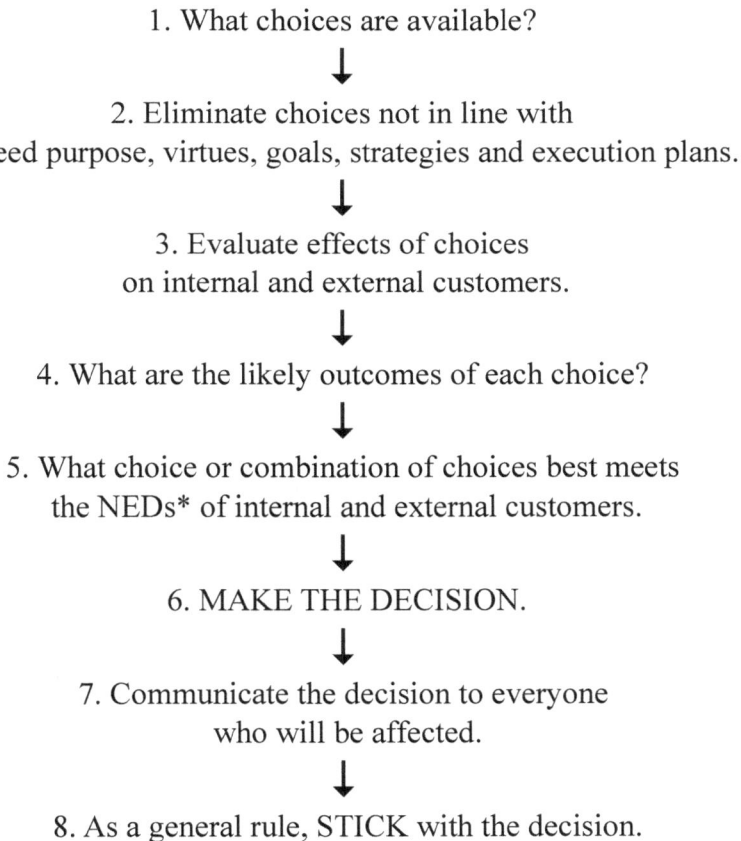

1. What choices are available?

↓

2. Eliminate choices not in line with
agreed purpose, virtues, goals, strategies and execution plans.

↓

3. Evaluate effects of choices
on internal and external customers.

↓

4. What are the likely outcomes of each choice?

↓

5. What choice or combination of choices best meets
the NEDs* of internal and external customers.

↓

6. MAKE THE DECISION.

↓

7. Communicate the decision to everyone
who will be affected.

↓

8. As a general rule, STICK with the decision.

---

*NEDs stands for Needs, Expectations, and Desires. In some quarters, must haves, should haves, and nice-to-haves, and in other places, demands, desires, and what is felt is deserved.

Possibility Actions:

To ensure decisions are made when and where it matters think and act on the following.

Have a decision-making process. It means good decisions are likely to be made and, crucially, it means transparency about decisions.

Map all transactions and interactions your business undertakes and provide learning and development for people so that they can make the right decisions at the right time without referring to somebody else. This also means you will be going a long way to meeting the needs that really motivate people as articulated by Daniel Pink:

> **Autonomy:**
> *the urge to direct our own lives*
> **Mastery:**
> *the desire to get better and better at something that matters*
> **Purpose:**
> *the yearning to do what we do in the service of something larger than ourselves*

We are the sum of the decisions we have made and those we haven't.

Decisions make or break us.

Are your decisions and the decisions of others making or breaking your business?

If you are an employee, take the initiative and volunteer to make the decisions you have the ability to make. Such authenticity will inspire confidence in you and will lead you to have more autonomy, greater mastery, and a strong sense of purpose.

Do your work.

Sparkenation 51.
Great service is normal.
Wooing and wowing
is an entirely different matter

Normal

Good service is what is expected.   It is normal.   The whole experience is what matters now.   Because we now have so many choices, as soon as we don't enjoy the experience, we go somewhere else.

I had to get up at 3.30 am on 31st March 2011 in order to catch a flight in Auckland New Zealand so that I could make a meeting in Melbourne Australia, so the night before I had an early dinner at Vapor's Holiday Inn near Auckland Airport.   Helen who served me did a great job and I told her so and also mentioned her name when I filled out the service questionnaire that is left on everyone's table.

When I got to the airport Virgin Pacific's computers were down. All their staff were great and handled a manual check-in well and we left on time.   Great service costs nothing except a little effort!

What Helen from Holiday Inn and the folk at Virgin Pacific did is normal and nothing whatsoever out of the ordinary.

Changing What's Normal

Wooing and wowing, however, is an entirely different matter and it is not yet normal.

The concept of *wooing and wowing* comes from my colleague Paul Dunn who is known internationally as 'The Wizard of Wow.'

The following are some of my thoughts on what woos and what wows:

Wooing is when

- ✓ a taxi driver you have never met before asks great questions about your travel habits and, on finding out that you travel regularly, offers to pick you up and provide you with a personal service.
- ✓ a coffee shop owner introduces themself and gets your name and shows, through conversation and actions, that they genuinely care about you.
- ✓ a hotel owner takes times out to find out who you are and what you do and how they can help.
- ✓ a conceirge person gives you insight you didn't ask for that enhances your experience.
- ✓ a colleague refers you to one of their major clients without you asking them.
- ✓ a friend remembers things that are important to you.
- ✓ a boss goes out of his/her way to find out about your family.
- ✓ a train conductor asks great questions about your travel.

Wowing is when

- ✓ the taxi driver who offered personal service actually delivers it.
- ✓ the coffee shop owner remembers your name next time you visit and continues the conversation you were having last time.
- ✓ the hotel owner actually helps you in what you do.
- ✓ the same conceirge person remembers your name and how they helped you last time when you return a year later.

- ✓ your colleague actually goes with you to meet their client.
- ✓ that same friend surprises you with a momento months later about what is important to you.
- ✓ your boss does something kind for your family without any expectation of getting something back.
- ✓ the same train conductor picks up where they left off the next time they see you.

Possibility Actions:

You get the idea.

Do your work.

Spend 20 minutes watching, listening, and paying attention to Paul Dunn's TEDx talk. The link to Paul's talk is in the vault www.changingwhatsnormal.com/vault/

"Human attention has become our principal currency."
Kevin Roberts, Worldwide CEO of Ideas Company
Saatchi & Saatchi

Are you paying attention?

Are you a lovemark?

Sparkenation 52.
Ensuring change programs
actually result in desired change

Normal

Most change programs result in little or no change and can even result in things being worse than they were before the program was undertaken.

I subscribe to many newsletters by change experts.   One newsletter I always get great value from is *Cultural Intelligence* by Steve Simpson and Stef du Plessis. In their August 2010 issue there are some great insights into why most change initiatives fail.

Changing What's Normal

Here are some of the insights explored by Steve and Stef:

Start out right by getting as many people as possible involved particularly those who will be affected by the change.

Build the urgency - everyone in the organisation needs to see the opportunity associated with the change - rather than being told about it.

Make everyone a choice-maker i.e. allow everyone to make choices and decisions.

Remove barriers and share successes.

I would add the following:

Bottom-up change is always more effective than top-down, therefore **ask** employees what needs to change in order for them to be better engaged.

Ask other stakeholders what needs to change in order for them to be better engaged and **do something about** the answers received when you ask.   Involve the people concerned, in the design and implementation of solutions.

Get outside help from experts to create strategies for changing, whatever it is your changing.   We can see what you can't because we do not have emotional involvement, however, **always involve the people who will be the executors** of your change program in the deciding of strategies.

Cascade strategies down to every individual performance plan therefore personalising the strategy and ensuring desired change is integral to daily work. This will also greatly increase buy-in and ownership and therefore make execution likely.

Ensure intrinsic motivators are met as integral outcomes of your change program.   As I have mentioned previously Daniel Pink's research clearly shows that there are three key intrinsic motivators: *Autonomy, Mastery, Purpose* These are outlined in sparkenation 50.

Possibility Action:

Together with all your stakeholders decide what you need to do to change what's normal in your organisation for the good of yourself, other people, our planet, and for profit where appropriate, and follow the advice above to make it happen.

If you are an employee, don't wait to be asked, rather, take the initiative and volunteer your feelings and thoughts. I know this is not normal!

Do your work.

Sparkenation 53.
We get what we give

Normal

It is normal to focus on what we get, more than on what we give.

Changing What's Normal

Since the GFC I have noticed and experienced greater scrutiny regarding return on investment (ROI) for providers of professional services like me. Indeed, each one of us is a Professional Service Firm whether we are a one person business or have employees, or work in someone else's business, and regardless of what we are offering.

Tom Peters first articulated this concept of being a Professional Service Firm in his book *Liberation Management* in 1992 and then in an article titled *'The Brand Called You'* for *Fast Company magazine* on 31st August 1997.

For me understanding and accepting that each of us is a Professional Service Firm is the first step to understanding how we can provide a return on investment for our clients/customers, and other stakeholders.

Do you see yourself as a Professional Service Firm?
(even if you don't have a business and work in someone else's business!)

What is the value that your clients/customers (internal and external) **demand, desire, and feel they deserve from you?**

As I have said, I sometimes call these the 'must haves', 'should haves', and 'nice to haves'. Today people want all three to feel that they have made a good return on their investment for our services.

Before I work with any client I follow the Alan Weiss formula - *agree with the buyer on objectives, measurements, and value*. My fee always depends on the value as perceived by the buyer.

What is your process?

The more we deliver the value to our stakeholders that they demand, desire, and feel they deserve, the less we will have trouble in demonstrating the ROI on our services.

Maybe I can help you

A few years ago I began to offer mentoring on skype to my clients as a standalone service, or as part of a package, and simply to demonstrate my value.

On most Monday mornings, wherever you happen to be in the world, I can provide a 30 minute mentoring session for free. All you need to do to book your session is email me with a date and time. When I am already booked I will email you back with alternative dates and times.

ROI according to Kevin Roberts = return on involvement

I had the privilege of hearing and meeting Kevin Roberts, the Worldwide CEO of Saatchi and Saatchi, in April 2011 at the National Speakers Association of Australia's annual convention. I have long been a fan of Kevin. His book *lovemarks* is one of my favourite books of all time.   You can tell that by the number of times I have quoted Kevin, right?

I took away much from Kevin's talk about the state and future of business and how to stand up and stand out which was the theme of the convention.

I was particularly taken by his insight that *ROI = return on involvement*. This idea really got me thinking and asking questions in the context of turning my brand into more of a *'lovemark'*.

Possibility Actions:

In the vault www.changingwhatsnormal.com/vault/ there is a link to a great ebook you can download by Tom Peters called *PSF is Everything*. I highly recommend that you study it and then act on what you learn in your own way.

Then answer these questions

Who really loves what you do?

Why do they love what you do?

What do you need to do to ensure your relationships with your stakeholders continue to grow?

What can you do that will encourage your stakeholders to be more involved with what you do?

How can you involve yourself in what your stakeholders do in ways that will add real value to them?

Do your work.

Sparkenation 54.
Other people don't rule the world, you do

Normal

"The road to hell is paved with good intentions."

Changing What's Normal

Two great facts of life are these:

1. Some things we can control
2. Some things we can't control

Stop worrying right now about things you can't control.
Start focusing on the things you can control.

Possibility Actions:

In the vault www.changingwhatsnormal.com/vault/ there is a link to an ebook containing 50 great differencemaking stories. **Read them all and get off your butt.**

Do your work.

I particularly liked Cindy Gallop's story. She founded *ifwerantheworld.com*

Cindy says: *"The single biggest pool of untapped natural resource in this world is human good intentions that never translate into action."*

Sparkenation 55.
Business may be
the last bastion of hope

Normal

Politicians talk all the time about the national interest and then serve their own, or their party's, interests.

Changing What's Normal

The result in the last national election in Australia means that Independents hold the balance of power.   In the interviews I watched, before the Independents chose which of the two major parties they would support to form a government, there was a notable absence of BS, unlike in the five weeks of the election campaign where BS ruled and community and country ran second and third to party ideology.

"Could it be that we were seeing the end of party politics?" I thought.

Parliaments should be about working together to ensure that local, national, and international interests are met.   Parliaments should be about collaboration not competition. The people who sit in our parliaments should be about enlightened self-interest, not self-interest or the interests of minority groups, or those who provide financial donations.

Sadly, BS returned very quickly to the Australian parliament when one Independent tried to hold the government to ransom by threatening to remove his support if they didn't do what he wanted to do in a particular area and everyone again started taking sides.

The problem with taking taking sides is it usually means winners and losers.

I have been involved in sport all my life for enjoyment, fitness, and the life-long friendships that have been the result, and because, in sport, having winners and losers is OK. It's the nature of games.

The same cannot be said for politics where the model of having a government and an opposition rarely means that the best ideas get adopted because unless the opposition agrees with the government great things rarely happen. In Australia recently, the government and the opposition fought over how to help people who had been devastated by floods and cyclones. It was appalling! The monumental failures in dealing with climate change and fixing the broken parts of the financial services system are just two more examples of the many.

The 2011 troubles in Egypt, Libya, and other places further demonstrate the problem with taking sides. I wish for democracy everywhere in the world, however, my kind of democracy means everyone wins or, at the very least, there is equity of opportunity.

Put religion into the mix and you often get more trouble, if this means people debating the undebatable about whose God is the right one and killing one another as a consequence.

Now I am not suggesting for one moment here that we don't take a stand against injustice, tyranny, inequality, or any other of the world's issues.   I am suggesting that we find better ways to live in our world.

Business may well be the last bastion of hope. Enlightened business leaders create shared value, i.e. everyone wins.

"Any business must make sense economically,
but there are now new imperatives.
It must also be environmentally
and socially sustainable over time.
The planet, people, and profits.
All for one and one for all.
We need to guarantee to our children that the foundations
are in place for sustainable enterprises across all dimensions."
him again, Kevin Roberts, Worldwide CEO of Ideas Company
Saatchi & Saatchi

Possibility Actions:

What are you doing in your business and in your life to create shared value?

The future is not about taking sides because the consequences of doing so are that there are winners and there are losers. The future is not about who is right and who is wrong. The future is not about politics or religion, although both have their place.

The future is about finding ways to live in harmony with each other and our planet, and where everyone has the opportunity to win.

The best way you can change what's normal in your life, your work, your home, your town or city, and your country, is to create shared value in all that you do.

What will you do that you are not already doing?

Do your work.

Be generous. Sparkenations 56 - 58

There is a new generation of people emerging where there are no age barriers or limits; 'Generation G' where the G stands for generosity. This is Sparkenation 56.

When we are generous we do things every day that amaze us, Sparkenation 57, and we are then in a space to co-create change where everyone can win, Sparkenation 58.

Sparkenation 56.
Are you a card carrying member of Generation G?

Normal

I read a lot online about Generation C (folk born after 1990) - *connected, communicating, computerized.*

I don't believe for a minute that 24/7 access to digital devices, as great as this is, means we are connected or good at communication. In fact the opposite can be the case.

We are in danger of losing both the art of real human connection and real communication, as well as the big C, in my view, compassion!

Changing What's Normal

While I accept the rise and influence of Generation C, I feel the rise of Generation G, where the G stands for generosity, will be a greater influence on the future of the world.

Possibility Actions:

> *"The small, brave act of cooperating with another person, of choosing trust over cynicism, generosity over selfishness, makes the brain light up with quiet joy."*
> Findings by Dr. Gregory S. Berns

In the vault www.changingwhatsnormal.com/vault/ there are two great links for you to check out; one to **find out more about Generation G** through an excellent post by *Trendwatching.com.*

The other link to explore is a **really practical way to embrace Generation G** by becoming a member, like me of *Buy1Give1 - giving businesses the power to change our lives* at *www.b1g1.com*

Please become a card carrying member of Generation G.

Do your work.

Sparkenation 57.
Do you do things every day
that amaze you?

Normal

Most people will believe it when they see it.

Changing What's Normal

The new world we are co-creating is about, as Wayne Dyer has said *"You'll see it when you believe it."*

I believe that the more we actually change what's normal, the more we see of what is possible in a world of infinite possibilities.

I love getting emails from my colleague Paul Dunn who often signs off with *"be sure to keep on doing things that amaze you."*

Possibility actions:

Here are 3 more ways you can do things that amaze you:

1. Little things make the big difference:

One of my favourite sayings comes from Anita Roddick, the Founder of The Body Shop. She said:
"If you don't believe little things make a big difference then you have never been to bed with a mosquito."

Take a look at all that you do for family, friends, and work mates and ask *"are they saying wow about my actions?"* Then change what you need to, so that all your actions are ones that mean people say *"wow."*

2. Embrace sustainability, it's actually simple:

Forget what other people are or aren't doing.

The monumental failure of various summits on climate change, and the posturing of some big businesses which are only interested in their own profit, can make sustainability seem complex and out of reach. Sustainability is actually simple. It means doing what we know we should.

Do the right thing by people and our planet yourself! And if you are in business, consider that building a business that is good for people and our planet can actually make you more money! Don't' believe me? Give me a call sometime. I can prove this beyond any shadow of a doubt. Don't forget there are 142 possible actions in my free ebook, *Differencemakers - how doing good is great for business*. Link to this download is in the vault www.changingwhatsnormal.com/vault/

3. Innovation is only possible when your culture allows it:

In conducting my research for my conference and event presentations worldwide it has become crystal clear to me that most business cultures make it hard for employees to turn information into insight into inspiration into ideas and therefore innovation, the successful implementation of an idea, rarely happens.

Does the culture of your business mean innovation is easy? And how about at home? Is innovation easy there too?

If you are doing what you've always done, most likely you are getting what you've always got. Is is time to change who you are, what you do, and how you do it? Do your work.

Sparkenation 58.
Change where everyone can win

Normal

The world is still primarily about winners and losers.

Changing What's Normal

I am often sneered at for being a dreamer and an idealist. Such derision warms my heart. I am equally derided for being a hard-nosed pragmatist. Such derision also warms my heart.

The new world we are co-creating is about being dreamers and idealists. It is equally about being hard-nosed pragmatists.

Possibility Action:

When my doctor came to see me to tell me I could go home following the weeks of recovery after the operation he performed that saved my life, he said: *"Don't die with your music still in you"*, a line sometimes attributed to former British Prime Minister Benjamin Disraeli, however more likely, from what I can tell, penned by Oliver Wendell Holmes.

I trust this book has inspired you to do your work. **You have special music that nobody else has, and you need to play it with all your heart** in order to change what's normal so that together we can move from a world of winners and losers, to a world where everyone and our planet can win. Do your work.

"It's not what the world holds for you.
It is what you bring to it."
Anne of Green Gables

Epilogue: Fulfilling Our Promise

In my year as President of the National Speakers Association of Australia Ltd (NSAA) in 2003/04 I chose *Fulfilling Our Promise* as my theme.

It was our Association's 16th year and I determined, after consultation with many members, and untold hours of soul-searching with fellow Board members, that is was time to change what was normal about how our organisation was going to get where we wanted to go. The process of changing what's normal became known as *Operation Stature* reflecting our desire to be an organisation recognised internally and externally as one of stature.

Operation stature is still a successful work in progress. Change never ends. It is usually both evolutionary and revolutionary, and often at the same time.

In my time as President, and ever since, as a part of my role as a mentor to my successors (a role all Past National Presidents fulfill) I have learned a great deal about changing what's normal. This experience, combined with working up close and personal on change initiatives and programs with many passionate and enlightened business leaders across a myriad of industries in several countries, has taught me that **fulfilling our promise is the great challenge of individuals, organisations, and countries,** and as we fulfill our promise we achieve our highest aspirations.

Fulfilling our promise requires continuous personal work, something I have entreated you to do at the end of each of my 58 sparkenations. All change is personal first.

As you continue to do your work you will **discover** more of the one-of-a-kind that you are.

Distinguish, develop, and **differentiate** yourself, and **deliver** and you will be indispensable.

Changing yourself, and then changing your relationships, will lead you to being loved.

You may be loathed by some, yet as you **connect, commune,** and **collaborate** with people with whom you establish a shared view, you will develop many relationships of high value and mutual reward.

The most powerful and productive organisational change occurs when we are continuously evolving and revolutionising ourselves and our relationships.   **Be aware, be clear, be inspiring, be attractive, be engaged, be authentic,** and **be generous,** in your organisation, and I have no doubt that you will play a major role in ensuring that your workplace culture is vibrant and that you and your colleagues will be making a major contribution to solving society's problems.

The result of change in your relationships, and in your organisation will lead you to achieving the great aspiration of being **valued.**

The result of changing yourself and change in your organisation will lead you to being **fulfilled.**

**I believe every human being wants and deserves to be loved, valued, and fulfilled.
Imagine our world when everyone is.**

Be the difference you want to see in the world. Do your work!
Be a sparkenator!
Global change is the result of all of our sparkenations.

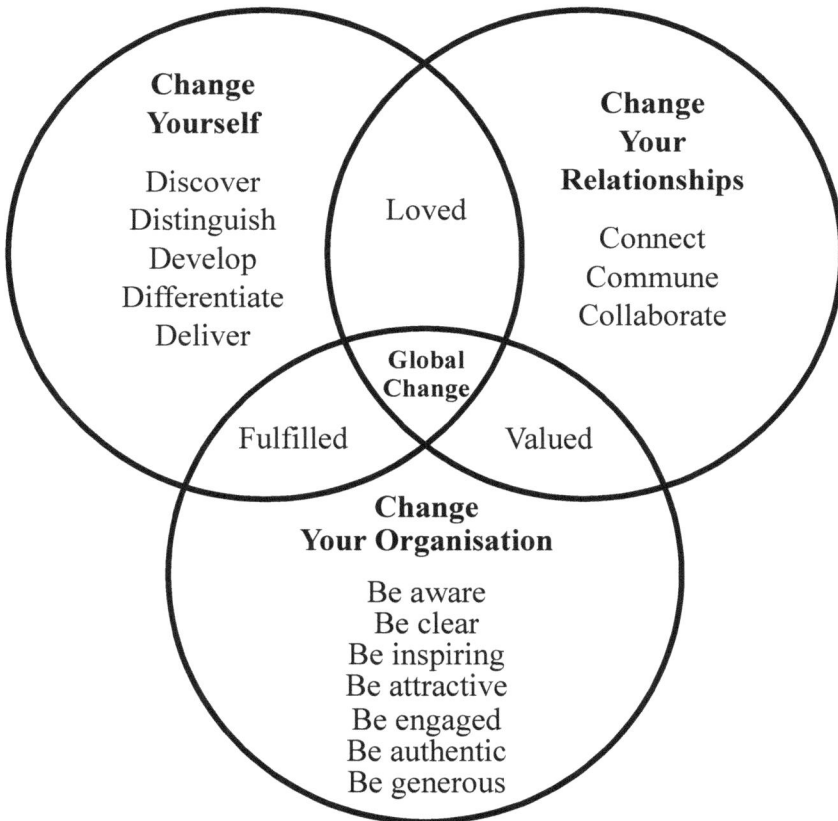

**Change
Yourself**

Discover
Distinguish
Develop
Differentiate
Deliver

Loved

**Change
Your
Relationships**

Connect
Commune
Collaborate

**Global
Change**

Fulfilled

Valued

**Change
Your Organisation**

Be aware
Be clear
Be inspiring
Be attractive
Be engaged
Be authentic
Be generous

Acknowledgments

I have been inspired and influenced by many people to change what's normal in my own life.

My heartfelt thanks to:

Gary Anderson, David Bernard-Stevens, Clive Bowers, Paul Gavin, Sara Knowles, Geoff McDonald, Terry McGivern, Rob McKenzie, Lily Newman, Richard Norris, Allan Parker, Gihan Perera, Julie Poland, Reg Polson, Gary Ryan, Simon Starr, Andrew Thorp, and Kwai Yu, who reviewed the draft of this book before publication and gave me the candid feedback I asked for.

All the writers whose books I highly recommend you read. Their details are in the notes and there is an extensive list in the vault. I am particularly grateful to Steven Farber, Seth Godin, Malcolm Gladwell, Marshall Goldsmith, Tom Peters, Daniel Pink, Kevin Roberts, Ken Robinson, and Alan Weiss.

Mike Vance for an inspirational speech over 30 years ago that caused such a sparkenation in my life that I changed my course and first began to discover my music.

Dr. Lionel Neri whose wisdom forever changed what's normal in my life.

The many members of the Global Speakers Federation who continue to inspire me to keep on becoming the best speaker I can possibly be. To mention you all would take another book! You know who you are. I am forever indebted to David Griggs who helped me to unearth my uniqueness and today keeps me grounded.

All the members of the *Differencemakers Community*. I am grateful for your courage and willingness to make a difference. I particularly thank Kwai Yu for his on-going inspiration and willingness to think and act outside the box.

Members of The CEO Institute and The Executive Connection in Australia, The Academy for Chief Executives and MD2MD in the United Kingdom, who became my friends/clients. Thank you for your willingness to explore things that matter, and for your inspiration through your willingness to do your work,

The few people who have accepted me for who I am and not tried to change me, yet by being who they are, have inspired me to continually be on the quest to do what I know I should. You know who you are. In particular I am eternally grateful for the friendship of Ann Blair and Terry Jenner AFL, whose travels to more than 40 countries with my wife and me, and untold hours of conversation, were not just great fun, they were integral to me in my quest to understand the world, myself, and to changing what's normal.

Finally I thank my wife Carol for her love, support, humour, and willingness to partner with me no matter what the possible outcomes. She is the great sparkenation in my life.

Notes

Prologue
Mark Sanborn quote from his article in 'Check under the hood' Speaker Magazine December 2010

Marcel Proust quote found at
http://www.brainyquote.com/quotes/quotes/m/marcelprou107111.html

Sparkenation 1.
Pink, Daniel; **Drive – the surprising truth about what motivate us,** Canongate, 2010 http://www.danpink.com/drive

Sparkenation 2.
Goethe quote found at
http://www.quotationspage.com/search.php3?Author=Johann+Wolfgang+von
+Goethe&file=other
The concept dates back to Greek Civilisation and the Pygmalion Effect. This is the origin of the Self Fulfilling Prophecy which Goethe and George Bernard Shaw and countless others have written about.

Sparkenation 6.
Joseph Campbell 1904 - 1987. Joseph Campbell Foundation has lots of resources http://www.jcf.org His book **The Hero with a Thousand Faces** helped me to change what's normal in my life and his interviews with Bill Moyers, The Power of Myth were also very influential.

Ken Robinson http://sirkenrobinson.com His book **The Element - how finding your passion changes everything** is on my list of the top 21 books I recommend you read. His TED talks are legendary. Sir Ken is in my view one of the leading thinkers of our time.

Steven Farber http://www.stevenfarber.com I think Steven's concepts of *do what you love in the service of people who love what you do* and helping other people to be *greater than yourself*, are brilliant.

Benjamin Zander http://benjaminzander.com Reading Ben's book **The Art of Possibility**, written with his wife Rosamund, awakened me to many things I had previously thought were impossible. Ben is one of the best speakers I have ever heard.

Distinguish: Sparkenations 7 - 10
Reference to 106 billion people found at
http://www.prb.org/Articles/2002HowManyPeopleHaveEverLivedonEarth.aspx

Sparkenation 8
Schwarz, Tony; with Gomes, Jean and Catherine McCarthy, Ph.D.; **The Way We're Working Isn't Working**, Simon & Shuster, 2010
http://www.amazon.com/Way-Were-Working-Isnt-Performance/dp/1439127662

Sparkenation 9
Goldsmith, Marshall; **What Got You Here Won't Get You There**, Hyperion, 2007. A great book. What impresses me about Marshall is his generosity in encouraging people to use his concepts. Many outstanding resources at
http://marshallgoldsmithlibrary.com

Sparkenation 11
Farber, Steve; **Greater Than Yourself**, Broadway Books, 2009
http://www.greaterthanyourself.com

Daniel Dennett quote found at Roberts, Kevin; **the future beyond brands lovemarks**, Murdoch Books, 2004, page 206.

Sparkenation 13
http://www.ashoka.org

Sparkenation 14
Do what you love in the service of people who love what you do is a wonderful concept from Farber, Steve; **The Radical Leap**, Dearborn Trade Publishing, 2004

Sparkenation 15
Oscar Wilde quote found at
http://www.goodreads.com/author/quotes/3565.Oscar_Wilde

Sparkenation 16
Burg, Bob; Mann, John David; **The Go-Giver** Penguin, 2007
http://www.thegogiver.com

Sparkenation 19
Passage found at
http://www.persistenceunlimited.com/2006/03/woody-allens-success-secret

Sparkenation 20
Tolle, Eckhart; **The Power of Now**, Hodder Headline Australia Pty Limited, 1999 http://www.eckharttolle.com

Sparkenation 22
Gandhi quote found at
http://www.quotationspage.com/quotes/Mahatma_Gandhi

Godin, Seth; **Linchpin**, Piakus, 2010; http://sethgodin.com

Sheahan, Peter: **Making $#IT Happen**, William Heinemann Australia, 2010; http://petersheahan.com

Church, Matt; Stein, Scott; Henderson, Michael; **Thought Leaders**, Harper Collins Publishers, 2011 http://www.mattchurch.com

Sparkenation 23
Alan Weiss' vast number of resources are at http://www.summitconsulting.com

Sparkenation 24
http://www.networlding.com/melissa-giovagnoli.php

Gladwell, Malcolm; **The Tipping Point**, Abacus, 2000
http://www.gladwell.com/tippingpoint/index.htm

http://www.networldingcircles.com

Details of Melissa Giovagnoli's books are at
http://www.amazon.com/Networlding-Building-Relationships-Opportunities-Management/dp/0787948195/ref=

Sparkenation 26
Mitchell is one of the most inspiring people I have ever met
http://www.wmitchell.com

Werbach, Adam; **Strategy for Sustainability**, Harvard Business Press, 2009
http://www.strategyforsustainability.com

Godin, Seth; **Tribes**, Piatkus Books, 2008 http://www.squidoo.com/tribesbook

http://www.linkedin.com/groups/Leaders-Cafe-2020-1764277?
trk=myg_ugrp_ovr

Sparkenation 28
No man is an island, entire of itself quote found at
http://www.phrases.org.uk/meanings/no-man-is-an-island.html

Sparkenation 29
You can find the **Spend Shift** book at
http://www.amazon.com/Spend-Shift-Post-Crisis-Revolution-Changing/dp/0470874430

Zig Ziglar quote found at
http://www.brainyquote.com/quotes/authors/z/zig_ziglar.html

Article by Michael E. Porter and Mark R. Kramer about Creating Shared Value (CSV) is at http://hbr.org/2011/01/the-big-idea-creating-shared-value/ar/1

Sparkenation 30
Roberts, Kevin; **the future beyond brands lovemarks**, Murdoch Books, 2004, page 158

Sparkenation 31
http://www.sethgodin.com/purple

The Book Rapper, Geoff McDonald. His details are in the vault.
You can find **The Culting of Brands** at
http://www.amazon.com/Culting-Brands-Customers-Become-Believers/dp/1591840279

Frank Nuovo quote, Pink, Daniel; **A Whole New Mind**, Allen & Unwin, 2005, Page 75

Sparkenation 34
Dr. Brundtland, the youngest person and first woman to be Prime Minister of Norway, is one of the world's elders. See www.theelders.org

John Elkington has been a major inspiration in my life
http://www.johnelkington.com

Sparkenation 36
http://en.wikipedia.org/wiki/Enlightened_self-interest

http://hbr.org/2010/03/leadership-lessons-from-india/ar/1

http://president.wbcsd.org

Sparkenation 37
Senge, Peter; **The Fifth Discipline,** Random House, 2006
http://www.amazon.com/Fifth-Discipline-Practice-Learning-Organization/dp/0385260954

Sisodia, Raj, Sheth, Jag, Wolfe David B; **Firms of Endearment**, Wharton School Publishing, 2007

http://www.awpagesociety.com/site/resources/page_principles

Sparkenation 38
Sinek, Simon; **Start With Why**, Portfolio, a member of Penguin Group (USA) Inc. 2009 http://www.startwithwhy.com

Nietzsche quote found at
http://www.brainyquote.com/quotes/authors/f/friedrich_nietzsche_3.html

Sparkenation 41
Harvard Business Review Reprint 96608 by Michael E. Porter
http://www.hbr.org

Samuel Goldwyn quote found in Roberts, Kevin; **the future beyond brands lovemarks**, Murdoch Books, 2004, page 90

Sparkenation 42
William James quote found at
http://quote.robertgenn.com/auth_search.php?authid=948

Pink, Daniel; **Drive – the surprising truth about what motivate us,** Canongate, 2010 http://www.danpink.com/drive

Sparkenation 43
Collins, Jim; **Good to Great,** Random House, 2001
http://www.amazon.com/Good-Great-Companies-Leap-Others/dp/0066620996

Kaoru Ishikawa http://en.wikipedia.org/wiki/Kaoru_Ishikawa

Sparkenation 44
Schwarz, Tony; with Gomes, Jean and Catherine McCarthy, Ph.D.; **The Way We're Working Isn't Working**, Simon & Shuster, 2010, page 4

Aon Hewitt study http://www.aon.com/attachments/thought-leadership/engagement_2.0.pdf

Blessing White report http://www.blessingwhite.com/eee__report.asp

Sparkenation 48
Desmond Tutu quote from The Elders website www.theelders.org

Sparkenation 50
Roberts, Kevin; **the future beyond brands lovemarks**, Murdoch Books, 2004, page 21

Dr. Paul Nutt's research http://researchnews.osu.edu/archive/decfail.htm

Pink, Daniel; **Drive – the surprising truth about what motivate us,** Canongate, 2010 http://www.danpink.com/drive

Roberts, Kevin; **the future beyond brands lovemarks**, Murdoch Books, 2004, page 33

Sparkenation 52
Steve Simpson and Stef du Plessis' Cultural Intelligence newsletter
http://ugrs.net/newsletters/CI127/pdf

Sparkenation 53
Tom Peters article for Fast Company magazine
http://www.fastcompany.com/magazine/10/brandyou.html

Alan Weiss' vast number of resources are at http://www.summitconsulting.com

Sparkenation 54
The road to hell is paved with good intentions quote found at
http://en.wikipedia.org/wiki/The_road_to_hell_is_paved_with_good_intentions

Sparkenation 55
Roberts, Kevin; **the future beyond brands lovemarks**, Murdoch Books, 2004, page 203

Sparkenation 56
Roberts, Kevin; **the future beyond brands lovemarks**, Murdoch Books, 2004, page 204

Sparkenation 57
Dyer, Wayne; **You'll See It When You Believe It**, Arrow, 1990

Acknowledgements
Mike Vance http://www.thinkoutofthebox.com/mikevance.html

Since 1990 Ian Berry has partnered with passionate and enlightened business leaders worldwide to change what's normal for the good of people, our planet, and for profit, through:

bespoke presentations and conversations that **stir** hearts, **shift** thinking, and inspire people to **step-up** their achievements. www.ianberry.biz/speaking/

and Heart-Leadership Events, Briefings, Programs and Mentoring www.ianberry.biz/heart-leadership/

Ian and his wife Carol live in Australia. They have been married since 1973. This is the partnership Ian is most proud of.

Ian attained the Certified Speaking Professional (CSP) designation which is the highest available to professional speakers internationally. He is a past National President of Professional Speakers Australia Ltd.

Ian has worked as a mentor with more than 1000 leaders, women and men, in over 40 countries.

He founded the *differencemakers community* in 2008. Subsequently this community evolved into the *Heart-Leadership Online Village.*

For Ian's latest sparkenations visit his blog https://blog.ianberry.biz/

Special Offers

Buy 100 books at a special price and Ian will spend a day with you in your business. **Your day will be tailored** to meet your needs, expectations, and desires and may include a seminar for your employees or customers, a workshop with your leadership team, a session with your Board.

Buy 250 books at a special price and Ian will spend a day with you in your business, tailored as above, **plus** he will provide a one hour, 1:1 mentoring session in person for up to seven people.

Buy 500 books at a special price and Ian will spend a day with you in your business, tailored as above, provide the mentoring, **and**, he will work a day in your charity or spend a day to help you to further a cause you are passionate about.

To find out more about these special offers please contact Ian direct on +61 418 807 898.

www.ingramcontent.com/pod-product-compliance
Lightning Source LLC
Chambersburg PA
CBHW071558210326
41597CB00019B/3299